Kundalini for Beginners

Awaken Your Kundalini Energy, Achieve Higher Consciousness, Expand Your Mind, Decalcify Pineal Gland

Elizabeth Wood

© Copyright 2020 by Elizabeth Wood. All rights reserved.

The work contained herein has been produced with the intent to provide relevant knowledge and information on the topic described in the title for entertainment purposes only. While the author has gone to every extent to furnish up to date and true information, no claims can be made as to its accuracy or validity as the author has made no claims to be an expert on this topic. Notwithstanding, the reader is asked to do their own research and consult any subject matter experts they deem necessary to ensure the quality and accuracy of the material presented herein.

This statement is legally binding as deemed by the Committee of Publishers Association and the American Bar Association for the territory of the United States. Other jurisdictions may apply their own legal statutes. Any reproduction, transmission or copying of this material contained in this work without the express written consent of the copyright holder shall be deemed as a copyright violation as per the current legislation in force on the date of publishing and subsequent time thereafter. All additional works derived from this material may be claimed by the holder of this copyright.

The data, depictions, events, descriptions and all other information forthwith are considered to be true, fair and accurate unless the work is expressly described as a work of fiction. Regardless of the nature of this work, the Publisher is exempt from any responsibility of actions taken by the reader in conjunction with this work. The Publisher acknowledges that the reader acts of their own accord and releases the author and Publisher of any responsibility for the observance of tips, advice, counsel, strategies and techniques that may be offered in this volume.

TABLE OF CONTENTS

INTRODUCTION 1

Chapter 1 *Knowing Kundalini* 2

    What Is Tantra 2

    What Is Kundalini 3

    The Benefits of Awakening the Kundalini 6

    The History of the Kundalini 7

Chapter 2 *Awakening The Kundalini* 10

    Why Release the Kundalini Energy 11

    The Central Channel 12

    Kundalini Yoga 13

    Meditation for Kundalini Awakening 17

    Breathing for Kundalini Awareness 20

    Using Crystals for Kundalini Awakening 25

    Using Essential Oils and Aromatherapy for Kundalini Awakening 29

    Dietary Essentials for Kundalini Awakening 30

Chapter 3 *Knowing When Your Kundalini Is Awakened* 33

    Physical Symptoms of Kundalini Awakening 33

    Emotional Symptoms of Kundalini Awakening 37

    Spiritual Symptoms of Kundalini Awakening 40

    Mental Symptoms of Kundalini Awakening 42

Chapter 4 *Kundalini And Your Chakras* 45

    The Path of the Kundalini 45

    The Seven Internal Chakras 47

Unblocking the Seven Chakras 53

Chapter 5 *A Changed Life After Kundalini Awakening*... **65**

    Increased Spiritual Awareness.. 66

    Freedom From Karmic Disturbances 67

    Open Psychic Ability... 68

Chapter 6 *Kundalini Misconceptions* **70**

    Kundalini Awakening Is Dangerous 71

    You Need Special Training 72

    Kundalini Is a Religious Practice 73

    Awakening the Kundalini Is Frightening..76

    Kundalini Changes Your Relationships With Other People 78

Chapter 7 *Healing With Kundalini* **83**

    Physical Healing With Kundalini... 84

    Mental and Emotional Healing With Kundalini..85

    Spiritual Healing With Kundalini...87

Conclusion.. **93**

Description **95**

INTRODUCTION

Congratulations on purchasing *Kundalini for Beginners,* and thank you for doing so.

The following chapters will discuss the Kundalini and its power and presence in your life. Waiting in a coil at the base of your spine is your Kundalini, the source of infinite energy that is present in all people. You are born with this energy inside of you, and it will die with you. In between birth and death, the Kundalini will wait for you to awaken it and utilize its power to help you realize your full potential physically, mentally, and spiritually. The power of the coiled serpent will fill your subtle body with energy and passion. When the subtle body is alive and well, the body will be balanced, and the mind will be peaceful.

In the spiritual teachings of ancient India, teaching held that the Kundalini was the meaning inside of everyone that would compel them to grow and evolve in their lives. These teachings have remained steadfast even today, and awakening the Kundalini and using it for one's benefit is the goal of many. This force that lies dormant within you until you call it forth will be the force that will elevate you into a profound consciousness and a profound spirituality. Awakening this power within you is a reality that you can come to know and enjoy in your own life. This reality will change your life in ways you can't begin to imagine. The Kundalini will express itself through you in the form of psychic powers, spiritual knowledge, and ultimate enlightenment. The transformation will bring you to great self-realization.

There are plenty of books on this subject on the market; thanks again for choosing this one! Every effort was made to ensure it is full of as much useful information as possible; please enjoy!

CHAPTER 1
Knowing Kundalini

Kundalini is known by many names, depending on the particular tradition that is referring to her. She can be Shakti, the mighty serpent, or the inner woman. In all practices, she is the energy that lies coiled at the base of the human spine, waiting from the minute you are born and staying with you until the minute you leave this physical world. It lies dormant in most people because most people either do not know how to awaken the energy of the Kundalini, or they are afraid of the power it might bring to them. But the strength of the Kundalini is a power that will lead you to spiritual liberation when you awaken it and learn to use it correctly.

What Is Tantra

Tantra is a term derived from another Sanskrit word, and it means 'expand the instrument.' While modern usage of the term usually refers to sexual matters, the traditional meaning of tantra is to expand the level of human consciousness to bring it to extraordinary heights, where the ultimate goal is self-realization. Tantra can also mean 'to weave,' which refers to the idea that the universe is an interconnected web of interrelated concepts and people. While tantra has many usages and many contexts, the most significant meaning of tantra is the use of the instrument to grow and expand the levels of consciousness. The practical and philosophical system of tantra teaches that everything that exists is divine. You are the instrument, and tantra wants to bring you to the level of the divine.

The universe is alive in tantra and not the illusion most people see it as. The ideals of tantra represent the physical manifestation of a joyful divine consciousness that is free from restriction. Tantra is a spiritual tradition that is body-affirming and world-affirming. Tantra will bring you to a level of spiritual liberation. It dissolves the division of the physical world from the spiritual world. Tools for your spiritual growth abound in every aspect of your life. Those who practice tantra desire transcendence above material existence. This transformation is not an extraordinary indulgence in regular life, but a constant focus on the divine. It works to promote divine consciousness through the activities in life. Your body is a living temple seeking divine energy.

While tantra is a practical system, it is also highly ritualistic and deeply devotional. Tantra was initially designed to help followers achieve the goal of moksha, which is a familiar concept in Hinduism. Moksha is the realization of liberating knowledge that leads one to acceptance of the self, or self-realization. This self-realization helps you to lose the focus on your ego and your body. You will then be able to focus on your divine self. Only Lord Shiva can bestow moksha upon you.

What Is Kundalini

The word 'Kundalini' is a term from the language of Sanskrit that means coiled snake. Sanskrit is an ancient language from the continent of Asia, in the area that encompasses India. Sanskrit is the primary language of Hindu teachings since it is regarded as the ancient language of Hinduism. The celestial Gods used Sanskrit to communicate with one another. The Sanskrit texts that speak of critical philosophical ideas and concepts of Hinduism spoke of the Kundalini and her power often. The concepts put forth in the Hindu teachings are also mentioned frequently in the teachings of Buddhism. Kundalini is a word that appears along with tantra, which is a concept present in both Buddhism and Hinduism.

Kundalini defines the source of the life force that everyone has within them. The consciousness and energy lie coiled against the base of the spine, present since birth. Kundalini energy triggers the formation of the child inside of the womb so that it can enter and lie coiled there. It is the inner fire of the human body, the ultimate force of life. Once the Kundalini is awakened, it arises in an energy that is like liquid fire, paralyzing, timeless, and electric. When you activate the power of the Kundalini, it will flow within you in the wavy shape of the serpent. It curves up from the base of the spine into your gut, past your heart, and into your head. The snake representation reminds you that the Kundalini can awaken either destructively or creatively, depending on the intentions within you, just as the venom of the snake can either destroy you or save your life.

In the traditions of tantra, Kundalini is known as Lady Shakti, the feminine side of the energy in the body. She is the one responsible for activating the strength and the power in the body. Her ultimate goal is the eventual meeting with Lord Shiva, who represents the masculine principle of consciousness. Together Shakti and Shiva manifest the full consciousness of the divine while displaying different sides of the same idea. The only time that creation, movement, and action can arise in the union is when Shakti and Shiva unite. The energy that Shakti brings is aimless and disordered. Energy will produce nothing by itself. It requires the direction, form, and content of consciousness. Without life, consciousness is nothing more than a dormant power that is incapable of accomplishing anything.

Shiva resides in the Crown Chakra, at the top of the head, the highest of the seven internal chakras. He represents compassion and the art of being grounded and centered. Shiva is aware of everything in the universe and operates with awareness, freedom, purpose, and direction. Shiva is the vital union between the external world and the inner world, and his power brings inner spaciousness and strength to you. Shakti, on the other hand, is powerful in her flexibility. She is free-flowing and fluid, and her energy is formless. The goal is to bring Shakti to her meeting with Shiva, uniting the Root Chakra with the Crown Chakra and activating all of the chakras in between them. Shakti rises when the Kundalini begins to awaken. The energy of Shakti rises through the seven internal chakras, awakening and balancing them, as she continues her quest to the Crown Chakra and the ultimate meeting with Shiva. When the two come together, the Kundalini is awakened, and energy and consciousness unite to transform you into a state of self-realization.

Awakening the Kundalini is a power that many people seek because of the awareness of higher consciousness and spiritual enlightenment it brings. Kundalini is a powerful force that fills your body with energy as it courses through the channel in the center of your spine. The life force that Kundalini brings to you is never-ending. It is inexhaustible. It will emit vibrational energies that you will become sensitive to in ever-increasing amounts. As your perception of the vibrational energies of the Kundalini becomes enhanced, your innate wisdom regarding life will grow and strengthen. You will enjoy a more profound knowledge of your role in the universe and your goals in life. The energy of the Kundalini will give you the power to seek knowledge, and this knowledge will provide more power to the Kundalini. It is an infinite circle of power and energy. The experience will add clarity to your life, and the transparency will assist in the Kundalini awakening.

As the energy from the Kundalini awakening gathers at the base of the spine, it will travel through the seven internal chakras as Shakti pursues her meeting with Shiva. Kundalini energy always seeks an upward path, and as it travels upward, it will open and awaken the chakras as it passes through. Kundalini is intelligent energy, and if it encounters a chakra, it can't pass through at that time, it will regroup at the base of the spine, building more energy for the next attempt. When the Kundalini energy has succeeded in opening the lower six chakras, it will complete its path to the Crown Chakra, where Lady Shakti will once again reunite with Lord Shiva. This reunion will complete the circuit of energy and will provide you with the physical, mental, and spiritual changes that you are seeking in your life. Then your subtle body will fill with conscious energy that is there for your use.

The Benefits of Awakening the Kundalini

Awakening your Kundalini will awaken all of the creativity within you. All of your significant accomplishments that are related to genius, creativity, talent, and grace will come from the awakening of your Kundalini. This awakening is the energy that inspires composers, artists, and poets at the same time that it inspires mathematicians and gurus and yogis. Any pursuit that requires creativity will benefit from awakening the Kundalini. This energy will carry those who awaken it to the goal of self-realization, which is the ultimate goal of life.

This abundant life force was first noted many centuries ago when the ancient scriptures spoke of the growth and ascent of the Kundalini energy. Awakening your Kundalini will connect you to the universe through your mind, body, and spirit. You will attain the full power of your nature and yourself. Creativity and wisdom will come to you with the awakening of your Kundalini. It will also provide you with a connection to the divine power that glows with the light of your consciousness. You will feel spiritual benefits on your physical plane. Your vitality and overall health will improve as the energy soars inside of you. Your capacity for joy and personal fulfillment will expand as the awakening enhances your consciousness. Awakening your Kundalini is a therapeutic practice, as well as a powerful spiritual experience. After your awakening, a divine light will shine from you, enhancing your moods and attitudes as well as your view of life. Kundalini awakening will give you the radiance that drives your inner glow.

All of your pain and distress in life comes from your mind. The lifestyle that most people follow creates patterns of negative thought that drive the vitality from your heart and your soul. Since this energy is the life force of all creatures, it resides in all beings until the strains of life force it down and destroys it. This level of negativity will force all of the vitality out of your soul and your body, leaving you feeling tired and listless most of the time. The negative thoughts that accompany this lack of energy will block crucial paths in your physical body, like the channel the Kundalini energy needs to rise to the Crown Chakra. The tools you need are found in your Kundalini energy. As you awaken this energy, you will become more conscious of your emotions and your moods, and you will be better able to govern your behavior correctly. The peak of your spiritual progress comes with the awakening of this power as it aligns your inner awareness with the awareness of the universe and the divine. You will achieve ultimate freedom with Kundalini awakening.

The History of the Kundalini

In early Eastern religions, it was taught that all humans were born with the energy of the divine, and this energy lay coiled at the base of the spine, looking much like a serpent. This mighty serpent was thought to be the sacred energy of all creation. It was taught that while everyone was born with it, few would ever know it since great work was needed to uncoil the serpent and release the energy to awaken the higher self of the individual and connect them to the divine.

Awakening the Kundalini energy inside is just one of the many facets of the practice of Kundalini yoga. Modern Western beliefs teach that yoga is a series of poses designed to bring grace, strength, and flexibility to the human body. While it is taught that these poses will bring peace and harmony to the spirit, most of the current practice of yoga in the Western world centers around learning poses. Learning poses is not the ultimate part of yoga. Traditional yoga involves learning and executing poses along with acceptable dietary practices, meditation, proper breathing techniques, the concentration of the mind, spiritual fulfillment, and ethical observances and guidelines. The ultimate goal of authentic yoga is to develop you from within, and the poses merely serve to teach you awareness of your body that will encourage you to be more aware of what you do to your body. You will want better dietary habits and a sense of inner peace. When you are mindful, you will make better choices and be aware of the consequences of your actions and how they affect the whole of you. Real yoga is a sacred union of your mind and your body.

Kundalini yoga is believed to be the forerunner of all other yoga traditions. Originally it was never taught publicly, only by private lessons. Before students gained access to the physical and spiritual lessons of the Kundalini masters, they were required to endure many years of initiation. The science of Kundalini was kept hidden for centuries, only shared in the small but elite community of disciples and yoga masters. Kundalini was a science of spiritual philosophy and energy long before the physical practice was developed. In the early teachings by the masters, students listened while the masters gave oral accounts of their spiritual visions. The yoga tradition developed as a physical expression of these visions. To the ancient masters, yoga was a sacred connection between the spirit and the body. The goal of yoga was the connection with the divine and not physical fitness. In the Kundalini tradition, the divine is creative consciousness and the energy from which everything flows. You can access the divine because the divine is already part of you and has been since conception. Kundalini is the method you will use to experience the true nature of your existence when you remove the false ego that causes you to be separated from the power and energy of the divine. In doing this, you will achieve self-realization through Kundalini awakening.

CHAPTER 2
Awakening The Kundalini

Try to imagine viewing the world around you with an expansive vision. Your keen powers of perception unite all perspectives into one image. You not only understand your feelings entirely, but you also understand the feelings and needs of everyone else. The judgments and decisions of others are now apparent to you. This awareness is part of the enlightenment that you receive when you awaken the Kundalini energy inside you. The story of Shakti and Shiva describes the energy as a dormant power coiled like a snake at the base of your spine. Envision a snake coiled at the bottom of a mountain, ready to uncoil and release its power at the top. Infinite energy waits within the snake. The serpent is the endless energy of the universe within you. It holds the force of creation, waiting to be utilized.

Awakening the Kundalini inside you is arousing the attention or awareness of the concentrated energy waiting within. This energy is not separate from your consciousness, but it merges with your consciousness when your mind is free from conscious thought. This freedom from thinking is needed for true enlightenment. You will open the spiritual channel of oneness and erase all duality from your life. Duality is seeing you as separate from the universe, man and nature. When Shakti and Shiva join, there can be no duality because their union brings spiritual awakening. This awakening is the correct path to happiness, and it is not conditional. It does not demand that your life will follow a particular direction. You will be one with all of creation. This transformation is the exalted state that is sought from a Kundalini awakening. You are now a part of everything and everyone. You possess an in-depth knowledge and higher energy levels.

Ancient students of Kundalini were taught to understand the ideas of Kundalini before they were ever taught any of the methods for awakening the Kundalini. The idea was to fully understand the results and the procedures before attempting the awakening. The primary objective was to release the full potential of human awareness from within. You will recognize your understanding, expand and refine your attention, and use that awareness to attain your unlimited self. As you clear your inner duality, cultivate inner peace and stillness, create the ability to listen and understand deeply, and maintain a level of excellence in everything you do in life.

Why Release the Kundalini Energy

Society pressures people from birth to think a certain way, feel a certain way, speak a certain way, and act a certain way. All of this forced suppression also suppresses your Kundalini, for it blocks the chakras that lie along the central channel and stops the progress of the Kundalini energy on its upward travels. When your energy, your life force, is awakened, you will impulsively express yourself in many ways you may not have used before. You will sing and dance, hug people and hold them close, express your wants and needs clearly, and feel the joy of being truly alive for the first time in your life. This ability for freedom of expression brings all life together in a magical experience of oneness.

When you live in full awareness, your energy will flow freely. This stagnant energy needs to be expressed so you can live a full life. Most people do not process their emotions completely, so they do not understand them. You probably feel angry or sad without knowing why, because you have suppressed the cause of that anger or sadness without confronting the event. People are often unable to laugh and cry, dance and sing, or express themselves freely because they have been suppressed from real feelings. You do this when you pretend to be okay, but you aren't, when you smile while you feel miserable inside, when you feel the need to force every reaction. As you begin this journey, you will collect energy that will likely be suppressed, for you have learned not to feel that way. As you gather more of this energy, you will find it increasingly challenging to continue hiding the real you. Most of your thoughts, emotions, and powers are locked in your subconscious mind, and Kundalini awakening will unlock them.

In time, you will no longer be able to pretend that this energy does not exist. Your repressed life will become more apparent to you and others. You will begin to see, with wide-open eyes, the lack of vitality and the hypocrisy, discomfort, disease, apathy, dullness, and misery that is controlling your life currently. Awakening the Kundalini will force all of these negative emotions to dissipate in the face of positivity and energy. Then you will fill with the power of the Kundalini energy as it rises through your central channel upward to your Crown Chakra. Then you will experience the transformation that will allow you to live in full awareness and self-realization.

The Central Channel

Everyone is born with a feminine side and a masculine side, creating three main channels of energy in your body. The right side is the masculine side, electric with energy. The left side is the feminine side, the magnetic side that seeks the power. The union of both sides occurs in the central channel. One of the steps to enlightenment through awakening the Kundalini is uniting the two channels of feminine and masculine into the central channel.

The central channel runs along the spinal column of the physical body. The spine itself is the physical manifestation of the central channel. This channel represents the presence of your soul, and it resides in all bodies. This presence is what created your body and what unites your soul and body together. The main internal chakras are located along the central channel.

Energy continually flows along your central channel. It moves downwards from your soul to your lower self and upwards from your lower self to your soul. This energy keeps you alive. Your soul uses this energy to drive your body and connect it to your soul.

The teachings of the ancient masters showed us that at the lower end of your central channel is the triangular form known as the Lotus of the Kundalini, where the power of the Kundalini waits, coiled like a snake, ready to awaken and rise. When your Kundalini awakens, it will rise through the central channel, level by level, passing through the seven internal chakras in its quest to reach the seventh chakra, the Crown Chakra, where Lord Shiva waits. When your Kundalini reaches this chakra, your soul will be freed from your mind and body. This freedom is the transformation that is the goal of awakening your Kundalini. You can't express your true nature without awakening your Kundalini.

Once you fully express the presence of the soul in your body, you will live life in a positive sense of wholeness. You will achieve complete awareness of the unity of your spirit with all matter, internal and external. Many different factors will work together to align your central channel and allow your Kundalini energy to rise to the top. You must be willing to use your entire being to awaken this energy since your whole being will need to be on the same path to achieve the transformation. All parts of you must work together to achieve spiritual enlightenment.

Kundalini Yoga

Kundalini yoga is a vibrant blend of physical and spiritual practices that incorporate meditation, breathing techniques, movement, and chanting mantras to achieve spiritual enlightenment. You will build increased consciousness and physical vitality. Your natural nature will unfold and grow during your practice of Kundalini yoga. It will help you shed the old you in favor of the new, more enlightened you. The ultimate goal is to unblock your chakras and silence your mind to increase your awareness of self. Kundalini yoga is an ancient art that mixes different practices to expand your consciousness. You will use the poses (asanas) along with chanting the sacred sounds (mantras), the breathing techniques (pranayama), with the cosmic energy (prana) to open your seven internal chakras and allow Kundalini to flow upward unimpeded. As your practice deepens, you will learn to unite with your cosmic consciousness and direct the flow of your energy where it is most needed in your body.

Everyone and everything you interact with is filled with energy. This yoga practice will awaken you to the power of your internal energy. It will guide you through the ups and downs in your life by helping you not overreact to situations. In the early days of its creation, Kundalini yoga was a study of spiritual philosophy and the science of energy, and it was taught to students by masters. The masters would spend years reciting their spiritual visions to the students before the students were allowed to progress further in their training. When Kundalini was brought to the Western world, all facets of the teaching became available to all people.

Kundalini energy is a tool you will use to achieve a life full of endless love along with joy, lightness, and inner peace. The yoga practice will make you aware of your body and how Kundalini will affect your emotion and energy. You have places in your body where your energy has stalled, locked places that prevent the power from flowing freely that interrupt the connection between your body and mind. These blocks will also prevent you from connecting with your higher potential and the universe around you. Kundalini yoga will cause the energy at the base of your spine to travel upward so your energy will flow, and your chakras will be open and balanced.

Kundalini yoga will build physical strength in your entire body. Each individual pose is held for an extended amount of time, sometimes for up to five minutes, so practicing this yoga is a great way to tone and strengthen your muscles. It is especially beneficial for building core muscle strength since many of the poses are done with specific breathing methods. Regularly practicing yoga will release the same hormones in your body that strenuous exercise will. The release of serotonin, also known as the happy hormone, will improve your mood. The release of hormones, along with the deep breathing techniques, will help to lower your blood pressure. The extended, deep, slow breathing techniques of Kundalini yoga will reduce stress and relax your nervous system. Cognitive function is impacted by the lowered stress levels and the release of beneficial hormones, boosting your memory and concentration. Since the core and the muscles around the diaphragm are strengthened, yoga will help with improving your digestion and speeding up your metabolism.

While all yoga sessions are different, each one will generally follow the same elemental composition. You will begin with an opening chant designed to warm and tune the body. Then the kriyas will be performed. A kriya is a pose or posture linked with a specific breathing technique. After all the poses are done, there will be a closing meditation of some sort. Teachers and students alike often wear all white clothing because white is considered to extend your aura and ward off negative energy. Kundalini is a more spiritual practice compared to other forms of yoga. As your power awakens, you will find that you are more spiritually connected with the universe and with yourself. You will experience internal peace, along with increased energy, charisma, creativity, and empathy.

The Lotus Pose is the right beginner pose for those wanting to try Kundalini yoga. It is a basic pose done while seated that helps to open your hips. This pose is a good posture for those who need to relieve tightness in the hip area but check with your doctor if you have any current hip issues. Sit on the floor and extend your legs out in front of your body. Keep your spine erect but relaxed. Get into a cross-legged position with your feet near your body and your knees pointing outward. If you can, cross your legs to put the left foot on top of your right thigh and vice versa. Sit and meditate as long as you are comfortable in this position.

The Cobra Pose is essential for awakening your Kundalini energy. Place your body flat on the floor on your stomach, with your feet and legs pressed firmly together. Rest the tops of your feet on the floor. Plant the palms of your hands firmly on the floor under your shoulders and push your upper body up to your waist. Keep your arms straight, and your shoulders and neck relaxed but upright. Hold this position for at least thirty seconds, longer if you can, and breathe deeply and evenly the entire time.

The Archer Pose is believed to make you feel strong and confident like a warrior. Stand upright with your spine straight but not stiff and your feet close together. Turn out your right foot, so it is at a forty-five-degree angle to your left foot. Step back with your right foot, straightening your leg while keeping your foot turned outward. Bend your left knee at a ninety-degree angle. Never let your knee extend out beyond your toes. Lift up your hands to the level of your shoulders while keeping your arms straight. Make your hands into loose fists with your thumbs pointing to the sky. Turn all of the upper body to the left and place your right hand on your left side just below the armpit. Hold still in this position for several minutes, and then repeat the sequence on the right side.

In other kinds of yoga, the poses flow with the breath, while in Kundalini yoga, the poses are combined with breathing and chanting. The purpose is to promote extended spiritual enlightenment, which makes Kundalini yoga a more spiritual form of yoga.

Meditation for Kundalini Awakening

Kundalini yoga meditation is not a religion, a belief, or the practice of magic. This form of meditation is nothing more than a simple technique designed to use what you already possess, which is your body, mind, and senses. You will use these to create communication between your body, your mind, and you. You will practice meditation to spend time with yourself in a relaxed atmosphere. This meditation is your time to connect with your breathing, to talk to your higher self, time to establish your rhythm, time to acknowledge and enjoy the life force in your body, and time to become more in love with your unique life circumstances. Meditation is your spending time with you.

Daily meditation cleanses your mind like a shower cleanses your body. This time is your opportunity to remain entirely in the present and clear your subconscious. Meditation will help you be kinder to others, healthier, better able to avoid mistakes, and more energetic. It allows you access to an opportunity to create stillness and calmness in your mind that will help you not react to the unceasing flow of thoughts from your mind. You can comfortably process your thoughts and feelings while you relax and rejuvenate your mind and body. This rejuvenation will help you to create a better rapport with those around you and handle stress more efficiently.

Do your meditation any time you feel alert and are ready to try. Some people prefer to meditate early in the morning when the world is quiet. Other people find that meditating just before going to bed at night helps to clear their minds of the events of the day. Although it is not recommended to meditate right after consuming a large meal since your body will be preoccupied with digestion, there is no one best time to meditate. The length of time you meditate is also your decision. Since every meditation works on a different part of the body or the mind, every meditation will be different. Begin with a time limit that suits your needs. You need to be comfortable with all aspects of your meditation, or you will not remain faithful to the practice. The first benefit of meditation is the opportunity to stop the activities of the day and spend a few minutes in quiet relaxation. Dress in whatever clothing is comfortable for you or no clothing if that is your preference. When choosing clothing, you might want to follow the ways of the ancient practitioners who considered meditation to be a special time. The dress they chose was clean, fresh, lightweight, and usually white. They often liked to cover their heads with a turban or a prayer shawl.

Before you begin or decide what technique to use, you will need to understand how to use your breath and how to use sound, as both are vital parts of meditation for Kundalini awakening. Meditation uses sound with rhythm to penetrate the thoughts and redirect their flow. Breaking through the patterns of emotions that are present in everyday thinking will help to elevate you. Choose a word or sound from ancient traditions or your language. The word you choose is not as important as the way you use it. One basic mantra in Kundalini yoga is the phrase '**sat nam**,' which means 'truth is my identity.' People will often use their chosen mantra during routine activities. When you chant a mantra, you are engaging in an energetic act that will stimulate the balance of your hormones while it engages your mind in peace and clarity. Chanting the mantra when you are not meditating will help to bring those feelings back to you.

Three languages of consciousness give you three ways to use a mantra. Chanting the mantra mentally or silently is the divine language of infinity. Whispering the mantra is the language of those who long to belong, like friends and lovers. A familiar speaking voice or a loud voice is the language that belongs to the world of humans and objects. Make your mantra more powerful, no matter how it is used, while you either actively listen to the sound or write the mantra on paper.

Meditations will also use breathing in different ways. You might break your breath into segments by chanting a mantra. You might use a specific pattern of breath by regulating your ratio of inhales and exhales. You might simply focus your attention on the flow and depth of your breath. Breathing is directly related to your energy levels and moods, so altering the pattern of breath or the rate and depth will also change them.

This process is one easy Kundalini meditation that you can use to begin your practice. Sit somewhere you are comfortable with your spine straight but not rigid. If you are sitting on a piece of furniture, do not let your back touch the furniture, but pose more upright. Keep your feet comfortably flat on the floor and relaxed. Lay your hands in your lap, with the left one under the right one. Lower your eyelids until your eyes are almost closed, but allow a thin line of light to come in. Keep your chest lifted to support your spine but relax your shoulders. Focus your entire attention on the flow of your breath while you breathe in and out through your nose only. Do nothing more than noticing your breath and how it moves in and out, how your body reacts to the flow of air. After focusing for a few minutes, consciously slow your rate of breathing. Normal breathing is fourteen to seventeen inhales and exhales each minute, so try to slow your breathing to eight cycles per minute. Listen closely to the sound of your breath as it goes in and out.

One thing many people struggle with when they first begin their practice of meditation is letting go of conscious thought and allowing the mind to clear. This mind chatter always sounds louder when you are trying to relax. This is an occasion where a mantra will help, like sat nam. Say or think **sat** as you inhale, and **nam** as you exhale. This mantra will help provide a place for your mind and breathing to focus. Let your thoughts come and go, not dwelling on any of them. Treat them as you would the background noise at work or a party. Stay with the sensations and flow of your breathing. Continue your meditation for at least five minutes or up to thirty minutes if you can. To end the meditation, stretch both arms to the ceiling as you inhale and exhale once profoundly and forcefully, and open your eyes.

Breathing for Kundalini Awareness

Proper breathing is vital for correct Kundalini Meditation and Yoga. The practice will help you cultivate awareness of your breath and integrate it into your daily activities. Yoga poses and meditation will be enhanced significantly by the effects of powerful breathing. It will release irritability and insecurity, improve your digestion, detoxify your body, cleanse your aura, balance the two sides of your brain, strengthen your nervous system, and clear your mind while it oxygenates your entire body. Proper breathing will also balance your energy with your life force.

There are basic breathing techniques that are part of Kundalini yoga, and it is essential to do them correctly to enhance your yoga practice. These techniques are implemented along with specific movements and postures to create powerful effects in your body. The essential breaths of Kundalini yoga are one-minute breath, passive awareness breathing, segmented breath, alternate nostril breathing, and breath of fire, suspend the breath, and long deep breathing.

Alternate nostril breathing takes advantage of the ability to breathe through either the right nostril or the left nostril instead of using both at once. Correct nostril breathing energizes you and alleviates unbalanced emotional and mental states as well as depression or irritation. Left nostril breathing activates your lunar energy and helps with your patience and letting go. You will do left nostril breathing to calm your nerves and mind and to help you relax. This breathing is particularly useful right before bedtime. To do either right nostril or left nostril breathing, simply block the other nostril with your finger or thumb and exhale and inhale long and deeply through the other nostril. You can also do alternate nostril breathing to create a balanced state that is both energizing and relaxing. Breathe in and out through one nostril first, and then the other.

Breath of Fire creates the amount of heat that is needed to stimulate and awaken the Kundalini. It activates your capacity to be centered in your body and your ability to focus. Breath of Fire also nurtures and energizes all of the systems in your body and oxygenates your blood. Breath of Fire needs to be performed correctly for it to work. On the exhale, bring your navel in toward your spine. The navel will automatically relax and go back out in the inhale. Focus on short inhales and exhales and let the inhale enter automatically; only the exhale is forced. Breath of Fire is a light, rhythmic, relaxed form of breathing. Try not to consciously engage the abdominal muscles because this will make your breath heavy and slow. Do not use or tense the muscles in your face, shoulders, or chest, and keep your ribcage relaxed.

One common mistake beginners make when doing Breath of Fire is to inhale actively. Doing this will slow your breathing because only the exhale is supposed to be active. The inhale and the exhale need to be the same length, but you will allow the inhale to happen naturally. You will know when you are doing Breath of Fire incorrectly because your entire upper body will feel tense. The first breath needs to be drawn long and deeply, to make you aware of how your body moves when you breathe. When you first begin Breath of Fire, only do a few and then stop. This will let you experience how it is done without the breath suffering.

Long deep breathing allows the energy and the breath to flow freely. To properly do this technique, you need to keep your spine straight. You have three separate zones of stretching in your spine that correspond to the three sets of muscles that will move when you inhale and exhale. You will facilitate deep breathing by stretching and aligning the spine in these three areas. To extend the muscles from the bottom of your ribs to your sit bones, pull your navel in slightly toward your spine to make your pelvis forward. Instead of leaning forward, your posture will be more upright. Sitting directly on your sit bones instead of leaning forward will facilitate your grounding with the earth as you connect more solidly with the floor underneath you. This position also frees the belly muscles to make them better able to do long, deep breathing. The muscles that surround your rib cage need to be strengthened and developed by raising them with your breathing. And the smaller muscles over your diaphragm will extend your breath so you can reach maximum inhale.

People will often cut off their exhalation prematurely, then try to initiate inhaling by using the small muscles in their upper chest instead of the muscles in their diaphragm. You do not need to emphasize the inhale to get enough air intakes. You will need to exhale if you are taking in a deep inhale fully. Before you begin your practice, spend a few minutes just observing your breath, to see if you put more force on the inhale or the exhale. With careful training, your diaphragm will automatically work to produce exhales and inhales, your diaphragm will grow more robust, and your exhalations and inhalations will lengthen significantly. This breathing technique will also help improve your vocal capacity.

Breath suspension is a technique for holding your breath during yoga poses. Suspending the breath means relaxing the muscles in your abdomen, ribs, and diaphragm. This technique will help support profound internal self-transformation. You should stop your breath on the inhale by first inhaling deeply, then lift your ribs slightly and relax your face, throat, and shoulders. Pull your chin in a bit, and sit still and calm. If you feel an overwhelming urge to exhale, just let out a bit of air to relieve the pressure. You can also suspend your breath on the exhale by first completely exhaling, then pulling the belly button back toward your spine. Lift your lower chest and let your upper chest relax. If you feel the urge to inhale, try to exhale a bit more. This technique will help you extend the suspension without struggling or straining for air.

When you suspend your breath, you are gradually reconditioning your nervous system. When you pause your breath on the inhale, it can temporarily increase your blood pressure, and suspending the breath on the exhale will temporarily lower your blood pressure. When you stop your breath, you are impacting the sympathetic and parasympathetic parts of your nervous system. These parts of the nervous system will activate during a perceived danger and then calm the body, respectively. Your brain knows to trigger inhalation when the carbon dioxide level in your blood is too high, which is what the brain responds to instead of oxygen levels. You can prepare to suspend your breath by taking several long inhales and then exhaling completely to rid the body of any excess carbon dioxide. It takes patience and regular attention to build this practice. If you ever feel disoriented or dizzy, then stop immediately, because this is not a sign of enlightenment. Pushing your body too far past its natural capacity will not help you.

With segmented breathing, you will divide your inhalation and exhalation into several parts. There will be a slight suspension of the breath that separates each segment, and each component will have a distinct beginning and end. This breathing method will stimulate your glandular system and your brain in different ways. The goal is for your breath to touch a particular area in the nasal passages to stimulate a specific set of nerves located there. You will keep your nostrils relaxed and direct your attention to the feel of your breath moving along the air passages. There are specific ratios for the rhythms in Kundalini yoga, and they all create a stable and predictable state of mind. Each rate has a particular purpose in your practice. If your inhale comes in four parts and the exhale in eight parts, that will help you let go of tension and calm your spirit. If the inhale comes in eight parts and the exhale only four parts, then that will energize you and help you to focus. When both the inhale and the exhale are eight parts, this breath is for centering and calming the spirit, and if both come in four parts, that breath will trigger alertness and clarity. And a breath with four parts on the inhale and one part on the exhale is energizing and uplifting.

Passive awareness breathing seems like a simple exercise, but it is a decisive step on the journey to enlightenment. Observing the act of breathing and how it flows in and out of your body will keep you calm and bring you back to the center. For real passive awareness, you need to be aware of your breath as it circulates through your body. Imagine your breath flowing into your lungs, part of it going up to distribute in your head, around your brain. More of the breath will flow sideways, out into your arms and hands. The remainder will flow downward, into your legs and down into your feet, coming back up to rejoin the rest of that breath so all can leave on the next inhale. This method is passive awareness of the breath, to follow the breath through your body calmly observing its path.

The one-minute breath is an excellent technique for calming your mind and body. It will help you feel open to the divine spirit. You will develop better intuition, and your physical brain will function better and more efficiently. Most people take between fourteen and seventeen inhales and exhales each minute. Someone who has practiced breathing may get that number as low as eight breathing cycles per minute, and a well-trained yoga guru will breathe just four breath cycles each minute. With the one-minute breathing technique, you will take only one breath each minute. You will inhale for twenty seconds, hold that breath for twenty seconds, and then exhale for twenty seconds. Don't try to do the whole twenty-second cycle on the first try, as you may need time to work up to this level. Try doing just five or ten seconds if you need to, and work up to the twenty-second cycles. When you can do it, you will feel the immediate benefits it provides. You will calm down quickly and be able to enter a state conducive to meditation quickly. If you can master this breathing technique, then you will be able to master every aspect of your physical and spiritual condition.

Using Crystals for Kundalini Awakening

Besides the central channel through which the Kundalini energy rises, there are other channels for energy to flow through in your body known as meridians. The channels are responsible for allowing the power of your life force to flow where it is needed. The meridians are all connected, so a blockage in one area of the body might be felt in another place. These blockages can be handled effectively with crystals. A jam will often appear as an ailment or a physical illness.

When you are awakening your Kundalini, and all of your attempts have been unsuccessful, it might be because one or more of your seven internal chakras is blocked. When this happens, the energy of the Kundalini will not be able to rise the top chakra, the Crown Chakra. Crystals are amazing for opening your chakras and eliminating the blockages that are keeping the energy from flowing freely through your central channel and the meridians. You can do this using just one crystal or a crystal in colors to match every chakra.

Your chakras reside along the central channel, and they connect your mind and body to your emotions and your spirit. If your chakras are blocked, you will experience issues and illnesses of your mind, soul, and body. Your chakras can become blocked for many different reasons, including emotional upsets, diseases, or problems with karma. Even issues that have their origin in past lives or childhood events can cause chakra blockages. Using crystals that will vibrate at the optimal frequency for each chakra will balance and align all of your chakras.

The easiest method to align all of the chakras at one time is to lie down and set a crystal on each of your chakras. You can choose a crystal that is associated with that particular chakra as the following list shows:

- Root Chakra – Smoky quartz crystal
- Sacral Chakra – Carnelian crystal
- Solar Plexus Chakra – Citrine crystal
- Heart Chakra – Rose quartz crystal
- Throat Chakra – Chalcedony crystal
- Third Eye Chakra – Amethyst crystal
- Crown Chakra – Clear quartz crystal

The cleansing process requires you to lie still for a minimum of ten minutes with the chosen crystal in place over the chakra it corresponds to. Focus on keeping your breath deep and steady, and meditate if you want to. So the Root Chakra crystal will be just beneath the Root Chakra, somewhere near the tops of your legs or right between them, and the crystal for the Crown Chakra will be located on the top of your head. Put the remaining crystals on your body at the place where the corresponding chakra is located in your body. Clean the crystals well after using them so they will be ready for the next usage.

If you do not own these specific crystals, then you can use other crystals from your collection. The process will work better if you use crystals that are in the colors that correspond with the individual chakras. Use the same method as above, where you put the crystals on or near the chakras using the following color chart:

- Root Chakra – black or red crystal
- Sacral Chakra – orange crystal
- Solar Plexus Chakra – yellow or gold crystal
- Heart Chakra – green or pink crystal
- Third Eye Chakra – violet or purple crystal
- Crown Chakra – white or clear crystal

You might not always have the perfect crystal or even a crystal in every color for every chakra. If all you can manage is two pieces of crystal to open your chakras, those two will be enough, as long as they are clear quartz crystals. This particular crystal carries the characteristics of every other crystal in the universe. A piece of quartz that is clear can be used in place of any crystal for any application. Since the crystals are multi-use crystals, they will need to be programmed for the purpose you want to use them for. After using an approved method for cleansing your crystals, hold them in your hands, and repeat your intention. Use a phrase that is simple but effective, such as 'I use these crystals to unblock my chakras.' Repeat this phrase several times. Then lie down and place one crystal near your Root Chakra and one crystal near your Crown Chakra, and follow the method outlined above.

Another method that works is the Crystal Point Method. For this method, you need a crystal point. This point is a piece of clear quartz that is flat on one side and pointed on the opposite end. You first need to cleanse the crystal. Then lie down on your back and hold the crystal in your non-dominant hand with the point showing. Begin at the Crown Chakra and make nine circles that spiral outward. The point of the crystal will move in the same direction as the clock moves while it hovers over the Crown Chakra. Then move your hand down to the Third Eye Chakra and draw a line back and forth from the Third Eye Chakra to the Crown Chakra by moving the crystal down, then back up, and then back down. Then repeat the clockwise circles over the Third Eye Chakra, rotating the crystal held in your hand nine times. Next, return your hand up the line to the Crown Chakra and follow the line up and down several times. Now follow a line down from your Crown Chakra to your Third Eye Chakra and then down to your Throat Chakra. Move the crystal up and down from the area of the Throat Chakra near to your Third Eye Chakra and then to your Crown Chakra, then return to the Throat Chakra and make the nine concentric circles.

Repeat this process for each chakra until you reach your Root Chakra. Always make the nine concentric circles, always moving in an outward spiral, always returning to your Crown Chakra to bring the energy down along the line of your chakras to the next chakra that is in line until all of the chakras have been balanced, all the way down to the Root Chakra. After reaching and completing the Root Chakra, lie still for a few minutes and mentally visualize the energy that is now flowing from the Crown Chakra down to the Root Chakra and back up the line to the Crown Chakra. Always cleanse the crystal after using it.

Using healing crystals will unblock your chakras to allow the Kundalini energy to flow freely through the central channel and then to your physical body through the meridians. The vibration of the crystals will also work with the life in your body to promote spiritual enlightenment and emotional, mental, spiritual, and physical healing.

Using Essential Oils and Aromatherapy for Kundalini Awakening

Essential oils are the distilled essence of the fragrance of plants, and they can be used to remove blockages in your chakras so that your Kundalini energy can flow freely through the central channel. If you are using this method, you must choose the scents that you like. The essential oil will not work if you don't like the smell and you either refuse to use it, or you don't believe in it.

When using essential oils on your skin, you need to use a carrier oil, which is an oil that the essential oil is mixed with to use. Essential oil is too concentrated to be put directly on your skin without a carrier oil. Choose your preferred carrier oil such as jojoba, almond, avocado, olive, or coconut. Mix a few drops of the essential oil into the carrier oil and rub it on your skin over the chakra that needs unblocking.

Another method is to rub your palms with the essential oil of choice and then wave your hands through the air to disperse the scent through the air around you.

You can also treat your environment by using an oil diffuser. This item is a small glass or ceramic bowl or vase-shaped object with a smaller neck and a wider bottom. There is a space underneath for a small candle to rest. Simply pour a bit of the essential oil into the bowl and then light a tea light candle underneath. As the candle warms the bowl, it will allow the fumes of the essential oil to escape into your room. Each of the chakras has specific scents that work best with that chakra:

- Root Chakra – frankincense, patchouli, myrrh, rosemary, sandalwood, clematis, and ylang-ylang
- Sacral Chakra – orange, rose, hibiscus, jasmine, and lady's slipper
- Solar Plexus Chakra – yarrow, chamomile, peppermint, juniper, vetivert, and marjoram
- Heart Chakra – rose, bergamot, jasmine, rosewood, holly, poppy, pine, and eucalyptus
- Throat Chakra – cosmos, trumpet vine, chamomile, sage, lemongrass, geranium, and hyssop
- Third Eye Chakra – lavender, spruce, frankincense, patchouli, clary sage, rosemary, wild oat, peppermint, and Queen Anne's lace
- Crown Chakra – lotus, frankincense, sandalwood, myrrh, jasmine, star tulip, neroli, benzoin, and lavender

Dietary Essentials for Kundalini Awakening

Kundalini awakening is a transformation of spiritual, mental, and physical practices that offer you an elevated way of thinking and living. While you chant, breathe, and pose your way to a higher spirituality, you might look for other ways to incorporate the ancient teachings of the Kundalini into other parts of your life. Your journey to self-realization can be significantly enhanced if you eat the correct kinds of foods. You need to treat your body as the temple it is in preparation for the union of Lord Shiva and Lady Shakti and the entrance of the divine power you seek.

Start eating healthier by cutting back on processed foods and any food that is artificially sweetened. These are more difficult for your body to process while it is focusing all of its energy on awakening your Kundalini. Whole grains, fruits, and vegetables will support your mind and body and your Kundalini awakening. Your diet should include only those foods that are fresh, simple, and whole. This diet will automatically eliminate any food that comes from a box or a can. Try to avoid meat and eggs as much as possible, since animal products will clog your meridians and make it difficult for the energy to flow freely. If you combine your whole grains, nuts, seeds, beans, fruit, and veggies in the correct amount, you will consume enough of the proteins, fats, and carbs that your body needs.

There are three main groups of yogic food. If you want to focus on sensitivity, intuition, discipline, peacefulness, and gracefulness, then you will need to consume a sattvic diet. If you're going to enjoy mindfulness, but your lifestyle is demanding or active, then you will need a combination of rajasic and sattvic foods. Those who embrace a demanding discipline, like Kundalini awakening and Kundalini yoga, require a variety of sattvic and rajasic foods. Everyone should avoid tamasic foods, as these are the foods that will prevent the enlightenment you seek. Tamasic foods are associated with anger, dullness, and impulsiveness, and they include eggs, fish, meat, and alcohol. Rajasic foods promote forcefulness and willpower with coffee, salt, warming spices, and stimulating herbs. Sattvic foods help you find lightness and clarity, and these include whole grains, legumes, fruits, and veggies, and for healthy fat, you will use ghee (clarified butter).

Eating healthy foods to improve your life and promote your practice is a good intention, but you may need some time to adjust your preferences. Remember, you are on a journey of enlightenment, so take the time you need to create your path to walk. The way you eat your food is just as important as what you eat. Keep your meals as simple as possible, with lots of fresh fruits and veggies. Eliminate sugar from your diet, unless it is the natural sugar that is present in your fruit. Bless your food before eating it, taking a few moments to spiritually acknowledge the blessing of energy the food will bring you. Eat slowly, taking the time to enjoy your food. Remove all distractions from the area where you are eating. And try to follow your meal with a short period of meditation. You won't want to indulge in a profound period of reflection while your food is digesting. Enjoy a short nap or sip a cup of hot coffee or tea while you relax for a few minutes.

You want to encourage your Kundalini energy to flow freely from its place at the base of your spine to your Crown Chakra. When Lady Shakti and Lord Shiva reunite, you will be able to project your awareness into the dimensions of the universe that are higher than the current realm where you reside. This reunion will provide you with an expansion of your consciousness that is indescribable and ultimately fulfilling.

CHAPTER 3
Knowing When Your Kundalini Is Awakened

The energy of your Kundalini lies in your nervous system and travels to all parts of your body. It is the energy force of your life, and it is regenerated every time you breathe. The ultimate purpose of awakening your Kundalini is to enhance your innate potential and awaken your higher ability. Everyone is born with a Kundalini that lies dormant at the base of the spine, and it must be revived so that you can reach your full potential. When your Kundalini is awakened, your chakras will open, and you will achieve true enlightenment.

The process you go through to awaken your Kundalini can be a fantastic experience, but it can also be a traumatizing and confusing time in your life. You will experience many changes during this time of deep purification. There are different methods for awakening your Kundalini, and all will help you achieve the self-realization you desire. You may wonder if your Kundalini is awakening based on the symptoms you are experiencing. It is easy to blame every sign on the awakening of your Kundalini, and while that may be true for some of the things you are feeling, there may be other reasons for your symptoms. Some of the symptoms you are feeling might be caused by mental or physical blockages you are experiencing. When you have strange symptoms, it is probably caused by the energy of the Kundalini trying to remove a backup so that it can flow freely to all parts of your body.

Physical Symptoms of Kundalini Awakening

As the energy of the Kundalini courses through your body, different issues, and sometimes pain, will arise in random areas. This feeling is particularly true in the areas where your chakras lie, or in the physical locations they are connected to. Today it is rare to find the person who has prepared for Kundalini awakening in the manner of the ancient students, but that is what is needed for a smooth transformation. Those ancient students endured years of strict dietary requirements and physical cleansing practices, only to be faced with learning to perform specific yoga poses and intense breathing methods. And along with all of this, they needed to learn obedience to their master and the system and let go of their egos. That kind of preparation is unheard of today as people either do not have the time to devote to the effort or they are looking for a quick fix. It is possible that you have done sufficient work in your previous lifetimes to allow you to reach spiritual enlightenment with a minimum of pain spiritually. But your physical body is new to this experience, since it was not with you in your past lives, and it will need to adjust to specific events during the awakening process.

During the awakening many different factors come into play, but there is mostly a gradual process as your psyche, physical body, and subtle body adapt to this new flow of energy. You need to be patient and take your time addressing your buried psychological issues and adjust them to the new patterns necessary to complete the Kundalini awakening. If you have heat in a particular area of your body, or pain that has no obvious source, this is probably the blockages in your body where the energy is stuck and can't push through. Since the needed clearing was not done before you began your awakening, you will need to make adjustments. During your transformation, you will not automatically get rid of your past habits, preferences, beliefs, and psychological issues. Some might disappear, but they will only be replaced by those that are buried deeper and take more time to uncover. All of these experiences will create blockages, and the energy will need to return to clear the blockages. You need to accept and let go of all of your old attachments and patterns if you want to achieve a real awakening. These old patterns are not the definitions of who you are, but they are past experiences that must be eliminated from your subconscious. Until you can do this, you will most likely feel divided, or you will wander in and out of positive awakened states.

If you feel pain in your shoulders and neck, you likely have a blockage in your Throat Chakra. Energy might become blocked here for several reasons. People have the habit of holding back their emotions or their self-expression. The words you have left unsaid are locked into the subtle energy field that surrounds the Throat Chakra. You might feel as though you are not allowed to feel angry if you want to achieve enlightenment, but this is not true. You are still a human being with human faults and feelings. You have emotions. You do not need to swallow or banish your feelings to be thought of as a spiritual person. You need to accept and acknowledge your feelings and learn to let go of them. Do not act on the emotion, but find a safe way to remove it from your consciousness without letting it get buried in your subconscious. Write your anger down and then discard it. Do yoga poses or meditate. Acknowledge the emotion and find a way to let it go.

You might also feel pain from an old injury that is locked in your subtle body and needs to be released. Kundalini energy will try to remove anything that is damaged or broken in your body. These are the blocks that prevent power from flowing freely. Your energy flow will become stuck in one area, or it will continue to return to one spot, trying to conquer a block created by an emotional or physical holdover from this life or one of your previous lives. It might even be related to an experience in the womb or during the birthing process. If you do not become immediately aware of the cause of a blockage, spend some time in quiet meditation and allow the memory to come into your consciousness.

The energy of the Kundalini coursing through you can cause a tremendous rush of energy up your spine. You might also feel tingling in other areas of your physical body as the power works through blockages and is released. You might wake up at random hours during the night, or be unable to fall asleep for hours. You might experience physical symptoms such as profuse sweating or crying for no apparent reason.

Since your spine and neck are the locations of the central channel through which the Kundalini energy runs, you might feel pain there as the power creates friction as it travels upward. You might have sharp pains in your neck or spine. These pains will subside as you work deeper into your practice. You might also experience headaches or sudden stabbing pains in your head. Part of this might be due to the tension in your neck and spine, and part if it is due to the energy of the Kundalini traveling to your Crown Chakra. Your sleep patterns may also be changed or disturbed. People who have transformed through Kundalini awakening usually do not need much sleep. This can cause you to be wide awake in the early hours of the morning for no apparent reason. Your body is now replenishing its energies from the energies of the universe. The cosmic energy flowing in your body means it will no longer be so dependent on material nourishment. The powers you gather from the universe will feed your soul and strengthen your immune system. You will also enjoy better health because the blockages that caused illness before are now removed. You may even begin to enjoy a more youthful physical appearance, which is mainly due to the internal cleansing and a reduction in your stress levels. You will rid yourself of emotional and physical baggage that alter your appearance and makes you look older than you really are. And you are now attracting a positive life force from the universe, which revitalizes your body and mind. This will give you a youthful glow.

You will experience some physical challenges that are caused by the clearing of blockages as the Kundalini energy moves through your body and changes your consciousness. Take advantage of your meditation and breathing, as well as your yoga poses, to help clear chakra blockages and restore the balance to your body and mind. Accept that this time might be difficult physically and move on with the realization that it won't last forever. Rest when you need to and consume a healthy diet to take care of your body. If you remain as calm as possible now, it will help you reach self-realization faster, so these symptoms will quickly subside.

Emotional Symptoms of Kundalini Awakening

During the awakening of the Kundalini, you might experience emotional symptoms that are not always positive. This transformation involves deconstructing your old self by peeling away all of the old layers of your consciousness and subconscious. You need to be reborn into a new consciousness, and you can't do this while you carry around old emotional baggage. Your ego will go through an experience that is much like death as you learn to transcend it. Once your Kundalini has awakened, your subconscious will break into your reality. You will not only be required to face all of your worst fears, but you will also face the fact that your reality is changing drastically. What you believed was the truth of your existence would no longer exist. You will know that everything within your reality was only an illusion created by your false hopes and beliefs, and this may be one of the worst experiences of your life.

Awakening your mental clarity by crumpling your old truth is the basis of a Kundalini awakening. You might go through an identity crisis of sorts as you find the things you once loved are no longer desirable to you. As you go through the process of being reborn, you will lose many of the old ideas you held onto so fiercely. Your emotions can feel like they are on a roller coaster. You will experience the extreme polarity of emotions moving from depression to euphoria and back again. You will feel like your emotions are entirely out of control. Part of this is due to the hormonal changes your endocrine system is experiencing. You will rise from deep waves of trauma that brings you to tears and find yourself on top of the world emotionally. As you are shedding your ego, your emotions will go through a state of disorder as they struggle to unite the mind and heart into one.

You might wonder if you are suffering from an identity crisis. You won't just feel lonely in your new world. You will feel confused about what is real and what truth is. No one around you will understand you, and you will have trouble relating to other people. A wall of isolation will build around you, and you will struggle to understand yourself and your desires. You will have difficulty determining who you are, what your goals are, or what reality means in your life. This feeling is disassociation, where you feel as though you are completely disconnected from experience and the people around you. You might believe that existence is a fabrication, and there is nothing real about your life. You may become mired in deep fear that everyone around you experiences in an illusion, and you will never learn to deal with material reality. This part of the process will be a dark time in your life, but it has a positive outcome because this is where your ego begins losing its control over you and your soul.

The shedding of your old ego is often referred to as the dark night of your soul. It is a natural part of the awakening process. Your aging skin is shedding off, and your old soul is being ripped apart so that you can be reborn into your new consciousness. As the old you resist the process of letting go, you will experience even more emotional conflict. The dark night creates a sense of isolation within you as your reality begins to crumble. You will recall past experiences that make you feel sad, either for letting them go or from having lived through the experience in the first place. You will spend a lot of your time digging up past events in your quest to rid your mind and soul of these old memories. You will remember what happened and think of ways you wish the event had been different, but you will need to let these things go. You might feel a sudden desire to make radical changes in your life, and these changes will affect any aspect of your life, from your job to your loved ones to your diet.

You will begin to see how the force of your mind is holding you back from realizing transformation. You will understand that your ego has always kept you trapped in the sense of preparing for the worst that might happen instead of hoping for the best outcome. You will see that it was all a ploy to keep your attention out of the present, where your actual energy lies. You will question many of the structures and systems that currently exist in your life. You will examine the traditions you held before, the religion and politics you put your faith in, and look for the actual reality in these things. You might feel a sudden deep need to work in the service of others, devoting your life to helping those who need help.

Sometimes you might feel a wave of extreme anger for the things you were denied for the things you never had or weren't given in your life. All of the pain you experienced will leave you unsettles and angry. Your anger will eventually subside into acceptance. You will realize your past experiences do not define the person you are now becoming. Each of your experiences was just a part of the journey of life, and you will be able to see all the past hurts as nothing more than bumps in your road. You will understand that your life was a reflection of the person that you were and not some terrible event that happened to you along the way. And you will eventually realize that you are ready to start living right now, this very minute and that you can't wait any longer to begin your real life. There will be certain people whom you can no longer tolerate because they either drain your energy or they give off unhealthy vibes. You will want to surround yourself with those people who think and act like you do, to help make your emotional transformation complete.

Spiritual Symptoms of Kundalini Awakening

The ultimate goal of awakening the Kundalini is to reunite Lady Shakti with Lord Shiva in your Crown Chakra to achieve true self-realization. When this happens, you might feel a sudden charge of energy in that chakra. Your perception will change, and you will see vivid colors all around you. As you enjoy your oneness with the universe, time will seem to stand still. You will feel many Kundalini symptoms like flashes of light and rushes of energy. You will know about things you never knew before, though your vivid dreams and your visions. It feels as though some higher power in the universe is downloading information into your mind through your spirit. You will begin to receive lessons for your walk through life and clues about your purpose.

You might feel more empathy for other people than you thought possible. You may feel as though you understand the feelings and emotions of others exactly as they are experiencing those feelings and emotions. This experience is a sign that your Third Eye has opened, and you are becoming more connected with the universe around you and your connection to it. And all of the old habits, relationships, and messes in your home will need to go. You will clean the house physically, which will help you to be clear spiritually. Those random feelings and emotions are just the leftovers of old events in your life, and you will want to be rid of them.

The new sense of oneness you feel with the universe will liberate you from many of your old possessive feelings. You will want to break free from worldly matters, and pleasures and material possessions may begin to lose their appeal. You will appreciate the inner harmony and peace that is part of your new spirituality. And these new feelings will drive you out into nature more. You will start to feel more at home when you are out in nature. This peacefulness is a sign that your Kundalini is awakening, and the energies of the universe are calling to you. The bountiful gifts of Mother Nature are attracting you outside.

Symptoms of Kundalini awakening might include an increased ability to know events well in advance of their happening, which means that your powers of extrasensory perception (ESP) have developed. This experience might come to you in different ways. You may become clairvoyant, experience telepathy, or increased intuition and vivid dreams. This increased ability is one of the most prominent spiritual features of the Kundalini awakening. This ability comes from your new connection to the universe through your Kundalini energy. And as you begin to sense the powers of other people, you will find that some people will draw you in, and others will immediately repel you. They might not ever say or do anything to you, but the vibrations that emanate from their auras will tell you all you need to know about them. The chakra cleansing that is part of your Kundalini awakening will elevate you to another level of consciousness that will give you the ability to detect energies from others as your energy senses it.

You might also experience memories of a past life or lives, as the case may be. As your long term memory begins to return, you will be able to know memories from your past experiences that have arisen from your subconscious. These memories have been deeply suppressed and are only coming to light because you have undergone a kind of cosmic cleaning with the rising of the Kundalini energy. These will appear as brief glimpses, daydreams, visions, or flashbacks. You will suddenly recall a past event with all of the emotions you felt when it was a current event. You will know this is a memory and not an event from your contemporary life, but the experience will be so vivid it will leave you momentarily confused.

Mental Symptoms of Kundalini Awakening

Any concept of how you currently view time will now change completely. You will operate from a more unified sense of perception for all events, whether they are in the past, present, or future, as your mind struggles to see things in the present. Time fluidly flows around you and does not seem to have structure any longer. Your consciousness will shift more to the right side of the brain where long term memory is processed and will rely less on the left hemisphere where short term memory is processed. The act of clear thinking might be more difficult right now, as your brain begins to think more spatially and less logically. You are learning to feel more and think less, and it is more difficult to channel your thoughts into neat little compartments as usual. As your Kundalini awakens, you will become more intuitive by nature as your right brains and left brain come together to give you ultimate clarity in a harmonious balance.

Your consciousness is rewiring itself so that all the actions of your right brain will be intensified. Your ability to experience life through what you see will be magnified, as well as your psychic abilities, spatial memory, and empathy. The left side of your brain will be less fierce as the right side becomes more vigorous. The left hemisphere dominates most of your thinking in the beginning since it controls your short term memory, powers of analysis, linear sequencing, problem-solving, and logical reasoning. You might feel that your brain is short-circuiting as your memory becomes weak and foggy, you may become unable to focus on simple tasks, and you become scatterbrained and forgetful. You might spend a good part of your time thinking words that you never say. You might feel overwhelmed by simple tasks or find yourself losing interest in things you once loved doing. You might try to force your logical brain to work harder as you fear that your spatial abilities in your right mind are gaining dominance. As the process of awakening the Kundalini progresses, you will find you can use both sides of your brain in a newly heightened awareness of the world.

You will feel disconnected as your consciousness forces you to look inside yourself for answers instead of always looking to outside sources. You will strive to attract the things that you seek with your mind and your relationships, and your interest will change as your frequency starts to shift. More aligned relationships that are more in tune with the needs of your soul will replace your old friends and connections. Your karmic bonds are beginning to loosen since you sometimes need to let go of things that hold you down if you want to evolve and grow. As your ego struggles to let go, you will meet with resistance, and it might manifest itself as turmoil, regret, and anger. You will find a greater understanding of yourself as you see the inner strength to seek the truth in all matters.

The reality, as you now know it will change, and you might feel as though there are two realities in your life. This shift is your state of consciousness, shifting, and evolving. You might feel vertigo when you are not moving. As your consciousness shifts between different states in other dimensions, the images and messages might invade your dreams. You will find it more normal to experience lucid dreaming and prophetic dreaming. You may feel a sudden urge to meditate. You will become more introspective, more comfortable with your thoughts, and you will no longer feel the need to share your opinion all of the time. Your powers of telepathy are growing, and this makes you more in tune with the world.

Thoughts and emotions begin to merge as your conscious mind undergoes a mental shift. Your perception shifts from a dualistic view of the world to one where you are thinking with your heart. You will now operate from a sense of empathy for others that give you a compassionate desire to help the world. You will swing back and forth between the attraction of the heart and the mind until you realize they can coexist and work together. Awakening the Kundalini will unify your mind and heart into one alliance. Your conscious mind is shifting into awareness of the present where the manifestation of reality is the greatest. You will acknowledge that your thoughts drive you and your truth into creating the kind of world you want to live in. Your actions will be fueled by your beliefs and intentions. When your ego finally dies, your life will change forever. You will see beyond the illusions of reality into the infinite connections that are there for you to make.

You will spend time reflecting on past events and past lives. Your mind and body will release the things that no longer serve them. The sudden desire you feel for going home is just your soul telling you to acknowledge your higher mind and higher self. Your connection to other worlds intensifies, and you can utilize the energies of the astral worlds around you. You will once again realize the unconditional love inside yourself.

All of the physical, emotional, mental, and spiritual changes you experience during your Kundalini awakening will prepare you for the fantastic new life you will live after the transformation. You will finally know your purpose in life. You will be gifted with new skills and abilities. All your past experiences will begin to make sense in the grand scheme of your life. You will feel a deep understanding of purpose, and you will no longer be the lost child you were before your awakening. You will know an overwhelming sense of peace and knowing that this is happening for a reason.

CHAPTER 4
Kundalini And Your Chakras

Kundalini awakening is a spiritual emergence of energy and consciousness that works through the system of the seven internal chakras. Each chakra has unique characteristics and holds material that drives your physical, mental, spiritual, and emotional beings. During a Kundalini awakening, all of this material will be examined, and some of it will be eliminated, as the awakening shows you what is needed and what is not. Your spiritual potential will begin to increase. You will navigate this robust process better by knowing what will happen and what needs to happen.

The Path of the Kundalini

The human body contains three channels through which energy flows. The Ida Nadi, the left channel, corresponds with the moon and the sense of darkness that the moon brings to earth. The left channel corresponds to your desires and emotions and the events of your past. When its energy is pure and clean, it represents the qualities of art, music, compassion, love, and deep joy. If your left channel is blocked, you may experience feelings of guilt, low self-esteem, depression, and problems with your emotional attachments. The Pingala Nadi, the right track, corresponds to the sun and the light and heat it brings to the earth. The right channel controls your planning and actions. When the right channel is open, you will feel emotionally healthy and stable. When it is blocked, you will feel hatred, anger, pride, arrogance, and have problems with egoistic behavior like selfishness. The central channel creates a balance between the left and the right track. The central channel allows the Kundalini to ascend through the chakras toward the Crown Chakra. This chakra is where the power that guides you consciously and unconsciously flows through. It brings you to your higher self-awareness.

The central channel extends from your tailbone at the bottom of your spine, where the Kundalini lays waiting to be awoken to the Crown Chakra, traveling along your spine. This channel is the channel of evolution and equilibrium. An open central channel is vital for maintaining an ongoing daily balance of energy. The central channel is the conduit for your autonomic nervous system, and it influences the involuntary functions that do not require you to control consciously. The autonomic nervous system tells your circulatory system to manufacture red and white blood cells, your digestive system to metabolize the food you consume, and your lungs and heart to breathe and beat. No matter what your attention is currently focused on, your body will continue to function automatically.

When you consciously switch your attention to your central channel during your efforts to awaken your Kundalini, your self-awareness will begin to evolve, and your attention will stop wildly swinging between current and past events. The left and right sides will start to lose their influence, and your attention will remain centered on your awakening efforts. You will experience real joy and inner peace by learning to exist in the present.

Your Kundalini energy has been present in your body since you were born, and it will remain with you until you die. It lies dormant in most people unless it is intentionally awakened in the pursuit of higher self-awareness. Your level of consciousness depends on the direction that your energy flows in the central channel. When your physical and emotional energy is lagging, that is a sign that your Kundalini energy is now flowing upward as it needs to flow. The Crown Chakra and the chakra just below it, the Third Eye Chakra, are spiritual magnets that pull the power of the Kundalini upward to facilitate a union with your higher self. Your ego is a magnet at the base of your spine that tries to pull the energy back toward it, taking you back into unawareness, selfishness, and negativity. The ego will draw your mind away from peaceful meditation by interrupting the flow of mindlessness.

The energy of the Kundalini lies coiled and asleep at the base of your spine. As it begins to awaken, it will rise through the central channel, past the lower six chakras, and into the Crown Chakra, where it will lead you into your higher consciousness and your real purpose. The awakening energy will work to energize the lower six internal chakras to make the way clear for the Kundalini to arise and travel upward. Your inner chakras are small circuits of energy that lie all along your spine. As your Kundalini awakens, you will gain new knowledge of your life and its experiences. The clarity that comes from this energy will enable more power to flow freely through your body. As the energy moves upward through the central channel, it will pass the chakras until it encounters a blockage, and then the power will work to remove the blockage so it can continue its upward travel. The Kundalini is intelligent energy, and it will do what is needed to open the chakras so it can attain its goal of spiritual awakening.

The Seven Internal Chakras

Of the seven chakras that lay along your spine, the lower three are physical, and the upper three are more spiritually centered. The chakra between them has characteristics of both physical and spiritual. Each of your chakras aligns with a particular color, and the colors follow the spectrum of colors that are found in the rainbow, and they also align with the colors that are found in your aura. For the highest chakras, a combination of colors is used that is referred to as iridescence or opalescence. Each chakra has a name and follows particular characteristics. Your chakras align with a specific part of your body and control the health of that part of your body. Your chakras will work together to balance the flow of energy in your body. Energy flows into the chakra and through them to each other. The process contains and regulates all of the energy that flows into and through your body. The intensity of the colors is directly affected by your health. A vibrantly healthy person will have an aura that glows with intense bright colors. The colors that represent unhealthy chakras will fade due to stress, anger, illness, or sadness.

THE ROOT CHAKRA – Muladhara --This chakra lies at the base of your spine and is the center of your basic needs, security, and your survival. The element of your Root Chakra is earth, and its theme is 'to be.' The Root Chakra governs your legs, feet, and bowels. Your Crown Chakra balances your Root Chakra in your body. Red is the color that represents the Root Chakra since it is an entirely physical color. Red promotes feelings of connection to the earth helps you feel grounded. The color red will make you feel alert, vigilant, and primal. This chakra is the very foundation of the entire system of energy inside your body. It is also the chakra that will store all of the excess energy for the other chakras. A blocked Root Chakra will give off definite symptoms. Your physical problems can include problems with the lower back, bladder, legs, feet, or colon. You might suffer from digestive issues such as irritable bowel syndrome. You can have weakness in your lower limbs, or you might feel ungrounded. You might be fearful, greedy, nervous, or possessive. You may harbor irrational fears about your safety, and you will probably have financial problems. Your Root Chakra controls issues linked to your survival, such as money, food, and independence.

THE SACRAL CHAKRA – Svadhisthana --This chakra holds the key to your deepest emotions and sensations. It controls how you express yourself and how you maintain your feelings inside your body. This chakra also controls your potential creativity as well as the balance of light and dark inside you. The Sacral Chakra is found deep within the lower part of your abdomen, just below your belly button. Its corresponding color is orange, and its element is water. The theme of the Sacral Chakra is 'to feel,' and it corresponds to the bladder, hips, kidneys, lower back, and the reproductive system. The Throat Chakra balances the Sacral

Chakra. A blocked Sacral Chakra will cause illnesses of your bladder, kidneys, or your reproductive system. Your emotions may be unbalanced, and you might feel shame and confusion over sexual matters or other intimate issues dealing with your body. This shame can include harboring feelings of guilt caused by things that make you happy. You might also use various addictions to make yourself feel better. Your Sacral Chakra is responsible for your sexuality and creativity. When this chakra is healthy, you will feel friendly, passionate, and fulfilled. You will exude feelings of pleasure, joy, abundance, and wellness. When you feel free to express your creativity and love for your body, then your Sacral Chakra will be open. A blocked Sacral Chakra will make you think creatively uninspired or emotionally unstable. Your Sacral Chakra is aligned with the color orange because this is the color of energy and creativity. Orange gives people a feeling of warmth and security, and they associate it with thoughts and feelings of pleasure, passion, and sexuality. You need to maintain personal equilibrium while allowing creativity, happiness, and emotions to flow freely to keep your Sacral Chakra healthy. Your Sacral Chakra grows more vital when you encourage a healthy, honest expression of yourself and deep emotional connection with other people.

THE SOLAR PLEXUS CHAKRA – Manipura -- This chakra is inside of the upper part of your abdomen, behind your belly button. This chakra is the place your inner fire begins and grows to ignite your self-confidence and willpower. Yellow is the color that is associated with the Solar Plexus Chakra, and its theme is 'to do.' Its element is fire, and it aligns with your spleen, pancreas, gallbladder, liver, and stomach. The Third Eye Chakra balances your Solar Plexus Chakra. You might experience problems controlling your emotions, and you may have low self-discipline when this chakra is blocked. You will either have an exaggerated sense of your self-importance or low self-esteem. You can alternate between feeling angry and insecure. Your body will struggle with gas, indigestion, bloating, fatigue, and weight control issues. The yellow color that corresponds with this chakra is intensely emotional. It will give you feelings of confidence and friendliness as well as courage, self-esteem, and optimism. The color yellow will make you feel prepared, capable, and stimulated in the same way that a healthy Solar Plexus Chakra will. This chakra rules your balance, self-esteem, and any action about commitment, personal power, and individual willpower. It governs anything issues with your digestive system, your stomach, and your metabolism.

THE HEART CHAKRA – Anahata -- This chakra is located in the center of your chest and is balanced by all of the other chakras. It is the link between the three lower, more physical chakras and the three higher, more spiritual chakras. Your Heart Chakra controls the way you express caring and love for ourselves and empathy for other people. The color that corresponds with the Heart Chakra is green, and its element is air. Your Heart Chakra aligns with your circulatory system and your lungs, arms, and heart. The theme of this chakra is 'to love.' A blocked Heart Chakra will cause issues with your circulatory system, your respiratory system, and heart disease.

You might often feel co-dependent, jealous, lonely, and sad. You will sacrifice your desires to be able to take care of other people. You might also hold grudges against others. Your Heart Chakra lies in the actual and metaphysical heart of your body. This chakra needs unconditional love to be able to function correctly at all times. When your life is full of discord, when you have suffered betrayal, when you feel unrequited love for another person or crushing grief, then your Heart Chakra will be blocked. The color green will give you feelings of good health and well-being. It fuels thoughts and feelings of kindness, compassion, and love, and will make you feel alert, healthy, and empathetic. Your physical self and your spiritual self will come together in the Heart Chakra. This chakra is where you will feel forgiveness, compassion, spiritual awareness, and love.

THE THROAT CHAKRA – Vishuddha -- Your truths are honored and expressed in your Throat Chakra. Located in your throat, the Sacral Chakra is its balancing chakra. Its corresponding color is blue, and its element is ether. Your Throat Chakra aligns with your jaw, thyroid, shoulders, mouth, neck, and throat. Its theme is 'to speak.' If your Throat Chakra is blocked, you might feel pain or tightness in your shoulders, jaws, or throat. Your thyroid gland may be diseased. You will either talk always or suffer through long periods of silence. You might think that lying is so much easier and find it difficult to speak the truth. You may have problems talking to other people or communicating your real thoughts and feelings. Your Throat Chakra is incredibly delicate, and excessively hearing other people tell you that your opinions are wrong or do not matter can cause damage to this chakra. If your expression is suppressed, it can cause you to hide deep within yourself or to close off all expression. Your Throat Chakra prefers open communication expressed with love and encouragement in a safe environment. Your Throat Chakra promotes feelings of intelligence and trust. Feelings and thoughts of logic, communication, and duty correspond with the color blue. This color can easily make you feel more smart, well-spoken, and efficient. Your Throat Chakra is the first of the spiritual chakras. A blocked Throat Chakra will cause you to have trouble speaking freely, staying focused, and paying attention when others are saying. It may also cause you to fear being judged by other people. When this chakra is blocked, it can also cause physical ailments like stiffness in the shoulders and neck, tension headaches, problems with your thyroid gland, and excessive sore throats.

THE THIRD EYE CHAKRA – Ajna -- Deep knowledge and intuition lie in your Third Eye Chakra. This chakra is located directly in the center of your forehead. Its theme is 'to see,' its corresponding color is indigo, and its unique element is light. This chakra controls your pituitary gland, the eyes, and the ears. The Solar Plexus Chakra is its balancing chakra. A blocked Third Eye Chakra will cause you to have trouble sleeping, which might include nightmares or night terrors. You might hallucinate or have strange visions. You will most likely suffer from headaches and will often be confused. Your sixth sense lies in your Third Eye Chakra, the reason that allows you to determine your feelings about other people and situations instantly. You will feel disillusioned by life when this chakra is blocked. To embrace your intuition, your Third Eye Chakra must be healthy and fully unblocked. All things that pass between you and the outside world must go through this chakra. An opened Third Eye Chakra will allow you to see what is real even if it is clouded by drama and illusion. When your chakra is blocked, you might find it challenging to learn new skills, use your intuition, recall important facts, or even to trust your inner voice. When your lower chakras are blocked, it can make the Third Eye Chakra blocked as well, and this might make you feel more judgmental, introverted, and dismissive toward other people. It can also make you feel anxious, depressed, and cause you to suffer from headaches and dizziness.

THE CROWN CHAKRA – Sahaswara --The highest of your chakras inside of your body is the Crown Chakra. It is where the source of the divine entity is found and is your connection to the spiritual world beyond you. The chakra is found at the top of your head. It is the goal of the Kundalini when it awakens, where Lady Shakti will join Lord Shiva. Its color is white, or violet and no element corresponds with it because it is above earthly connections. The Crown Chakra directly controls your cerebral cortex, which is responsible for processing language, personality and intelligence, gross and fine motor function, and the operation of your senses and your pineal gland, which is responsible for the regulation of all of the hormones in the body. You might have migraines or be sensitive to bright light.

You may have mental illnesses that involve delusions. You will suffer from mental confusion, chronic fatigue, and fog, insomnia, nightmares, or night terrors. You will be greedy, materialistic, lonely, and disconnected spiritually. Your sense of the self will be limited and very rigid. You will think narrow-minded thoughts and keep yourself isolated from other people. Your ego might be out of control because you lack any feelings of compassion and care toward other people. Its theme is 'to understand,' and the Root Chakra balances the Crown Chakra. If this chakra is blocked, you might have problems with your spirituality. You may deny the existence of any sort of higher power. You may become overly opinionated or feel as though you do not connect well with other people. You will probably struggle to understand spiritual concepts, and you might even fear anything that has to do with spirituality and mysticism, such as the occult or religion. You will not have access to your higher powers if your Crown Chakra is blocked. The colors of the Crown Chakra, violet and white, stand for spirituality, oneness, and meditation, as these are the ways to enable access to your Crown Chakra. It is possible to live with a blocked Crown Chakra, but you will never be able to feel genuinely spiritual or be one with the universe.

Unblocking the Seven Chakras

You possess an energetic body, as well as a physical body. All of the energy pathways in your body are fed from the central channel, from the awakened energy of the Kundalini. The word 'chakra' means disc or wheel, and this is how the chakras are pictured, energetic little wheels spinning inside your body from the force of the energy of the Kundalini. Each of the seven chakras located along your spinal column has a unique name and different correspondences.

Besides having a physical realm that it powers, they also have crystals, colors, scents, foods that assist the chakras in staying healthy.

The Root Chakra represents all of the things that make you feel secure and safe. It means your basic needs for food, money, shelter, and survival. Your Sacral Chakra governs your sexuality as well as your creativity, pleasure, and sense of well-being. Its health will determine how well you will handle new experiences. This chakra is also the basis of many of your emotions, so it will determine how deeply you are willing to feel. Your self-esteem, self-worth, and self-confidence are governed by your Solar Plexus Chakra. An open chakra in this area will give you a strong will and determination. Your Heart Chakra determines the depth of the joy you feel in your life and your empathy for other people. Your Third Eye Chakra governs your imagination and intuition. The Crown chakra connects you to the mysteries of the universe.

The energy from the Kundalini will travel through the central channel, past these chakras. When it flows through your chakras, it will lead you to an expanded state of consciousness and awareness. Awakening your Kundalini will lead you to an understanding of your higher self in your new self-realization. But the Kundalini can't move through the chakras if they are blocked. The energy from the Kundalini will help to unblock the chakras, and there are other things you can do for each chakra to free it and assist in your Kundalini awakening.

Root Chakra -- This is the foundation for your overall health and well-being.
Red is the corresponding color of the Root Chakra. Picture a pool of the color red covering the base of your spine. Imagine this pool protecting and warming your Root Chakra. See this pool flowing down your legs and grounding you to the earth. Surround yourself with the color red by wearing red clothing or putting out red accessories in your home. Use those essential oils

that have an earthy essence like sandalwood, frankincense, or patchouli. Burn some incense of these scents or put some essential oil in a fragrance diffuser. Your Root Chakra likes foods that are red and any of the root vegetables. Fill your kitchen with beets, carrots, apples, cherries, and onions. Surround your home and outdoor space with healing red or black stones like smoky quartz, jet, hematite, garnet, red jasper, bloodstone, or red carnelian. Your Root Chakra loves movement, so dance to your favorite music. Do different yoga poses like downward dog, warrior I and II, and Mountain Pose. Go outside and enjoy a walk. Feel all of the energy that you receive from nature and the earth. If you can walk around barefooted, then that is even better. Do some work in your yard or plant a garden. Join events in your local community or get out and meet your neighbors.

Write down in a journal the things that make you feel supported in your life, or what you need to help you feel supported. Think about how strong your roots are. Note any time you think negative thoughts about yourself that limit you and your abilities. Write down new goals you want to achieve and note areas where you might need to be healthier. When your Root Chakra is strong, you will have a strong foundation. This foundation will help your health and add to the stability of your other chakras. Your confidence and energy will increase as your Root Chakra grows stronger. You will no longer be driven by fear and guilt. You will finally know that your life is going according to your plan and that everything will work out just fine.

Sacral Chakra -- this is the internal center of your sexual, emotional, and creative energy. If you pay attention to your actions, thoughts, feelings, and the physical sensations of your body, you will know when to cleanse and balance your Sacral Chakra. There are many signs that this chakra needs healing. You might have disorders of your stomach, kidneys, or lower back. You overthink everything, or your creativity is stagnating. You might be emotionally aloof or extremely sensitive. You feed on other people's drama. You have no energy and are always exhausted. You suffer from reproductive or sexual issues. You might either feel absolutely no emotion, or you might be overly emotional in any situation. You are addicted to feeling pleasure, and you find it wherever you can, in drink, food, drugs, gambling, work, compulsive shopping, or any other area you can find to do something to excess.

When your Sacral Chakra is healthy, then you will feel comfortable with yourself just the way you are. Take some time to explore your creativity with activities that make you happy. Explore new activities that look like they might be fun by trying something you have not done before. Look into activities like quilting, drawing, cooking, sculpting, making jewelry, photography, or sewing. Remember that some creative crafts take more time to learn than others, so be patient with yourself if you find a new activity you enjoy doing but aren't very good at in the beginning. Put effort into any new activities you try. Think about the ideas you heard about sexuality as a child and decide which ones no longer fit your lifestyle. These ideas might be what is blocking your Sacral Chakra so take the time to get to know you better and learn the things that make you happy.

Emotional holes in your life will cause you to try to fill them with something to make you happy, and this is how addictions begin. Try to think about where your thoughts and feelings were when you became addicted to whatever habit you might be fighting. Please spend some time learning what it is you are trying to hide from or what you lack in your life. Take ample time to think about your emotions and your emotional triggers as these may be the key to what drives your addictions. Surround yourself with the color orange, the color that corresponds with the Sacral Chakra. Wear a piece of jewelry or a garment that is orange colored. Lay orange throws or pillows around your home. Eat more orange-colored food like apricots, mangos, oranges, carrots, papaya, sweet potatoes, and peaches. Even setting out a bowl of nectarines, oranges, or tangerines on your kitchen counter will help.

Embrace your body as it is now and stop hating the way you look. Make changes if you are not happy with the way you look, but accept yourself as you are first. Explore guided meditations for body affirmations. Experiment with different healthy foods and ways of eating. Add grated ginger to hot dishes or drink ginger tea. Join an exercise class or learn to do yoga, especially goddess pose, camel, butterfly, pigeon pose, reverse warrior, and cobra. Meditate with guided meditations or daily affirmations. Use essential oils to clear out blockages in your Sacral Chakra like jasmine, neroli, bergamot, rosewood, orange, and ginger. Choose a movie or a book that is not the type you would typically choose. These activities will help unblock your Sacral Chakra while you are learning to live your life.

Solar Plexus Chakra – because this chakra will shine brightly like the sun when it is unblocked, it is sometimes referred to as the lustrous gem of the energy centers in the human body. When your Solar Plexus Chakra is freed, you will feel self-confidence, self-control, and a tremendous inner drive. Unfortunately, many mindsets, habits, and traumatic experiences in your life can cause this chakra to become stagnant, suppressed, or blocked. This suppression will also happen if you suffered from emotional, sexual, physical, or mental abuse at any time in your life, but mainly as a child. This chakra is the center of your self-esteem and your willpower. This chakra aligns with the element of fire and is responsible for regulating all of your energy that is associated with your vitality, identity, intention, and action. You will know if your Solar Plexus Chakra needs healing by paying attention to your physical sensations, as well as your actions, feelings, and thoughts.

Essential oils will help unblock your Solar Plexus Chakra, especially rosemary, cinnamon, sandalwood, clove, cypress, and black pepper. Wear a diffusing pendant as a piece of jewelry, put a few drops into an oil diffuser in your home, or wear a bit of diluted essential oil of your choice on your wrists. Specific crystal will also help you to unblock this chakra. Wear the crystals as jewelry or carry them with you. The best options are the tiger's eye, citrine, topaz, yellow calcite, and amber. Different culinary herbs will help you unblock your Solar Plexus Chakra. Use lemongrass, rosemary, ginger, marshmallow leaf, or chamomile in your cooking or to make a great tasting tea. And certain foods will bring balance and health to this chakra. You will want to focus on eating more whole grains like oats, rye, spelt, and rice. Your diet should include a lot of legumes like beans, chickpeas, and lentils. Spices will help to warm your body, so focus on using cumin, ginger, cinnamon, and turmeric when you cook. And certain yellow vegetables and fruits such as corn, bananas, pineapple, and lemons will help you to feel better almost immediately.

Avoid overly critical people. If you can't cut ties with them entirely, then try to limit your contact with them. Spend time with supportive people who will help to build you up. Spend some quiet time getting to know yourself and what it is that you want out of life. You need to know yourself. You will grow and develop when you are honest with yourself. Usually, those people who have a blocked Solar Plexus Chakra will spend a lot of time suppressing or avoiding things or fighting against them. And get rid of any anger that you are storing inside of you. Doing so is a great way to unblock your chakra rapidly. When you release the stored anger, you will have plenty of room for energy again. Use positive affirmations for guided meditation whenever possible. Break free of unhealthy attachments by asking yourself why you are holding on to these useless and outdated ideas. If an object, memory, desire, or belief is not serving your highest good, then get rid of it.

Heart Chakra -- this is the center of your love and unity. When your Heart Chakra is unblocked, you will feel forgiving, receptive, open, generous, accepting, and connected to other people and yourself. If this is blocked, then you will feel fear, bitterness, resentment, loneliness, and social isolation. As the center of your balance, love, and connection with other people, the Heart Chakra is responsible for regulating the energy inside of you that is associated with self-love, self-acceptance, openness, compassion, and love for other people that is unconditional.

Green is the color of the Heart Chakra, so start spending more time outside in nature. Get out to any place that is lush with greenery. If you live in the city, then try growing a small garden or fill your home with house plants. When your heart is balanced, it is beautiful, and it shares its loving and kindness with others freely. Try some loving meditation to heal your Heart Chakra. Don't be afraid to set personal boundaries. Set personal limits, and do not be scared to say 'no' to other people. You can't make yourself happy if you only try to make others happy. Take better care of yourself and your heart by learning to be gently assertive.

Herbs like astragalus, nettle, hawthorn, angelica, hops, holy basil, and rose are the best ones to clear and open the Heart Chakra. Drink them as a soothing tea. The energy of individual crystals will help you to unblock your Heart Chakra. Carry or meditate with green fluorite, ruby, chrysocolla, emerald, rose quartz, prehnite, rhodonite, malachite, and jade. Certain essential oils like neroli, lavender, ylang-ylang, angelica, rose, and marjoram will heal this chakra. And green foods added to the diet will significantly enhance the health of your Heart Chakra. Try chard, pears, green apples, celery, grapes, broccoli, lettuce, kale, zucchini, peppers, cabbage, avocados, peas, spinach, and kiwis. And try different yoga poses for cleansing, especially camel, eagle, cat, fish pose, cobra, and forward bend.

When your mind is overly judgmental, then it won't be easy to show love for others. Clear these thoughts from your mind. Permit yourself to feel love for yourself and others. Your emotions are meant to be embraced and used, not repressed, shut out, or controlled. Allow yourself to be bored, sad, jealous, angry, or unhappy as you need to be. And become accustomed to the feeling of a hug. Learn to hug others and let them embrace you. Do not push away the love that others want to show you. Don't deny compliments or affection, but accept them graciously. Practice counting your blessings and don't take life and love for granted. Try to be a more thoughtful person. Use those affirmations for guided meditation if that helps you to become more loving. Use phrases that begin with 'I love,' 'I nurture,' or 'I open myself.' And don't forget to laugh as often as you possibly can. Laughter is one of the best healers that you have available to you.

Throat Chakra -- unblocking this chakra will make you more honest, creative, assertive, confident, and not afraid of expressing your truth. If the Throat Chakra is blocked, you will struggle with problems such as untrustworthiness, stubbornness, dishonesty, verbal aggressiveness, lack of creativity, social anxiety, shyness, and a fear of expressing your thoughts. If your Throat Chakra is blocked, you might be unable to express your real thoughts and feelings. Your Throat Chakra is the chakra that is responsible for regulating the energy inside of you that is associated with understanding, creativity, and authenticity.

Use affirmations with your guided meditation to heal this chakra. Use phrases that begin with the words 'I feel,' 'I am,' and 'I think.' Since the Throat Chakra is especially receptive to both of these, hum mantras or uses sound therapy. Keep a private journal of your deepest feelings and thoughts. Write something in your journal every day, so you will be in the habit of expressing your feelings. Blue is the corresponding color of the Throat Chakra so add into your diet those foods that are blue such as blackberries, blueberries, grapes, currants, and plums. Some foods that help unblock this chakra are pears, lemons, apricots, grapefruit, apples, figs, peaches, and kiwis. Fennel, echinacea, slippery elm, cinnamon, clove, spearmint, and elderberry are some of the herbs that will help to heal your Throat Chakra. They are best used for making soothing tea.

Surround yourself with anything blue in color. Stare up at the sky or out at a body of blue water. Wear blue clothing and toss blue blankets and pillows around your furniture. Use the energy of appropriate crystals like tanzanite, larimar, azurite, lapis lazuli, aquamarine, and blue kyanite. Yoga poses that help unblocks this chakra are lion pose, plow pose, and fish pose. And surround yourself with the scents of essential oils like neroli, ylang-ylang, myrrh, eucalyptus, rosemary, clove, and frankincense. And always try to drink pure water. Practice deep breathing to ground yourself. Calm yourself with deep breaths that will help to center you. While you are practicing your breathing, silently give thanks to your life and the universe for supporting your life. Breathe slowly and deeply while you focus on listening to other people and the words that they are saying. Singing, screaming, and laughing are all good ways to release excess built-up energy that might be stuck in your throat. Laughing or crying allows you to let go of frustrations and negativity. And singing is probably the most beautiful and natural way to open your Throat Chakra. Anyone who can speak can sing, so turn up the volume on the radio and enjoy yourself.

Third Eye Chakra -- The energy center in your body that is responsible for your intuition, thought, manifesting, perception, and reality is your Third Eye Chakra. When this chakra has opened, a doorway to spiritual enlightenment is opened. When this chakra is balanced and clean, then you will possess emotional balance, self-awareness, insight, strong intuition, and clarity. If this is blocked, then you will struggle with mood disorders, mental illnesses, paranoia, depression, anxiety, cynicism, and closed-mindedness. You need to explore new points of view if you want to unblock this chakra. This curiosity will help you break the cycle of being close-minded and rigid in your beliefs. You will also be easily lost in delusion and fantasy if you are not grounded in reality. Try to work on being present in your everyday life and do not allow your mind to wander off too far.

Get outside into the sunlight every day. Sun will help unblock your Third Eye Chakra because it will help you clear your mind. Use basil, saffron, blue lotus, rosemary, lavender, jasmine, passionflower, star anise, or mugwort herbs in cooking or as incense. These will also make delicious teas. Add more purple foods to your diet like purple kale, purple cabbage, purple potatoes, purple carrots, blueberries, blackberries, eggplant, raisins, figs, dates, and prunes. Use Third Eye Chakra appropriate essential oils like sandalwood, clary sage, vetiver, juniper, frankincense, and patchouli. Amethyst, kyanite, lapis lazuli, labradorite, sapphire, and shungite crystal can be worn as jewelry or carried in your pocket. Work on your yoga poses, especially the child's pose, head-to-knee poses, dolphin pose, and standing forward bend. Light a candle and set it three to four feet in front of you and stare mindlessly at the flame. Keep your vision focused in a comfortable, natural way. Try to be more self-aware, as this is a necessary skill that you need to develop. It will help you to build your self-awareness. Keep a private journal of your deepest thoughts and feelings. Stand outside at night under the full moon. And always tell yourself how well you are doing. Use positive affirmations with your guided meditation to unblock your Third Eye Chakra. Use phrases that begin with the words 'I trust,' 'I see,' or 'I create.'

Crown Chakra -- The highest chakra is the Crown Chakra. It is the energy center of your consciousness on a cosmic level and the ultimate goal of the Kundalini during awakening. The

Crown Chakra connects you to all things eternal because it is the seat of your divine awareness. It is the goal of Lady Shakti as she rises to meet Lord Shiva in their lasting union. You will easily connect to your higher self when this chakra is unblocked. When this chakra is blocked, you might suffer from neurological and endocrine disorders. Your Crown Chakra is your access to enlightenment and the window to your soul. Your former sense of isolation will be replaced by being connected with all of humanity. You will feel more playful, light, and fluid as you become less rigid and begin to lose your ego. You will live in the moment more fully and be better able to see the big picture of life. Your reality will be defined by serenity and expansiveness.

One of the best ways to unblock your Crown Chakra is by meditation. Use your affirmations as guided meditations. Do not become too immersed in your thoughts but let your ideas flow freely. Find a quiet place to relax and turn your attention inside to yourself. Break out of the comfort zone you are in and expand your limiting thoughts by reading books or watching movies that you usually would not choose. Identify those areas of ignorance or prejudice that you need to change. As you spend more time hearing and reading the thoughts of others, you will have less time to dwell on your limiting beliefs.

Simplify your surroundings to declutter your life. Mental and emotional distress is caused by and aggravated by an excess of mess. When you simplify your environment, then you will also be purifying yourself. By cleaning the external environment, you make it easier to clean the internal environment. When you have made space available, then you will have room to create a space for your daily spiritual practice. Create a small area that is the place where you will go to get in touch with your spiritual self. Put things there that mean something to you like crystals, candles, incense, books, or stones. Take stuff from around your house that is meaningful to you and put them in your special place. Your spiritual practice will be uniquely yours. You might do yoga, rituals, pray, read, study, sing, meditate, or simply be. Spend time talking to whatever being you feel most drawn to, like the Ancestors, Goddess or God, Soul, Spirit, Life, or Spirit Guides. Prayer is very beneficial and very simple. Look for signs the Spirit is speaking to you. You will need to be open to the guidance that is happening all around you. If you are feeling cynical, then you will cut the ties between your surroundings and your mind, body, and soul. Question any beliefs you have held all your life and make the changes I needed. Cynicism usually comes from a sense of worthlessness and insecurity. Work to overcome your low self-esteem. Don't forget your affirmations for guided meditation. Always use phrases that begin with the words 'I see,' 'I am,' and 'I trust.'

The Kundalini must rise past the chakras on its path to awakening. The chakras can't remain blocked if the Kundalini is to rise to its quest of the Crown Chakra. The Kundalini and the chakras need to work together to experience self-realization. Use any method that works for you to facilitate the flow of healing energy up the central channel to aid in your transformation.

CHAPTER 5
A Changed Life After Kundalini Awakening

Once you have awakened your Kundalini and made it through the transformation, your life will change forever. It will then be time to decide how you will integrate the new you into the old life and make the two work together in harmony. Awakening your Kundalini is something like setting your insides on fire and burning out all of the old you to make room for the new you. Old ideas and beliefs are gone in favor of new truths and beliefs. All of the old psychological garbage you wrapped around yourself like a blanket is now gone, and you feel peace and calm in its place. This new feeling is alive and wonderful; you just aren't sure what to do with it.

Human beings are amazing creatures. You will be a fantastic person when you learn to get out of your way then. You will flow towards the people and things that support you and are meant for you. You will need to grow up all over again after your Kundalini awakening. Everyone who experiences the transformation will walk a different path because the journey is personal. You have cleared out space inside of yourself that was full of unpleasant thoughts and unwanted old experiences. Your soul will intuitively want to live its best possible life. Once you have begun the adjustment process, then you can take the actions you need to take to start to move toward your new life.

In your new life, after the awakening, you will fail and succeed, and this is normal. You are learning to manipulate your divine intelligence. You have no control over the process, and you can't predict how it will go. Sometimes life will flow on its own, and other times you will need to take action. You will alternate between receiving what life offers and giving back to others. You will make mistakes, especially in the beginning. Be patient; everything will work itself out.

You will find you are more aware of life going on around you, and you will be more sensitive to the people in your environment. You will develop a deep relationship with your soul, and you will need to pay more attention to your powers of intuition. The opinions of others no longer mean as much as they once did. Spend some quality time every day with your deeper self, taking time to look beyond your ego and your personality. Use any tools you need to allow yourself to evolve and heal.

Increased Spiritual Awareness

Spiritual awakening is a personal experience. Your entry into self-realization might be a gentle glide, or it might be a rough jolt. It might happen gradually, or it may come on you like an explosion of energy. You might experience some of the signs of an awakened Kundalini like vivid dreams, hearing sounds, or seeing flashing lights. This awakening experience will be one of the most memorable and radical experiences of your life. The reaction you have to the awakening will depend significantly on where you were emotionally and spiritually before the awakening. You might feel this is one of the worst experiences ever, or you might see this as the blessing you have been expecting. You are reborn in the transformation, and your ego is dying and letting go. The world as you knew it would be wholly transformed, and you will realize that the things you sought so desperately in your life were right before you all the time. You want to share your experience with those close to you and help them see what you know now, and you will be confused when they do not seem to understand what you are telling them. A spiritual awakening is impossible to understand unless you have experienced one yourself.

Those you want to share with may not understand what you are telling them. You might fear being judged by others and find it difficult to describe. You might want to keep the experience entirely to yourself, and that is fine too. Those around you will know that something is different, but they will not know what it is. But you will see the self-realization that comes from real awakening. You will eventually learn to trust the inner voice of enlightenment. And you will see that this enlightenment is not a goal or an achievement. It is a point where you gain awareness in the world beyond yourself. Trust in your spiritual growth so that you will continue to grow. If you doubt your change, you will prevent it from happening. And don't be afraid to apply the spiritual progress you now have to your life to create a new experience, for awakening your Kundalini was to achieve a transformation in your life.

Freedom From Karmic Disturbances

Every human is comprised of three bodies. You have the physical body, the astral or subtle body, and the karmic or causal body. Each body has its energetic field of numerous densities that vibrate at different frequencies. The karmic body operates at the lowest frequency, but it is the most expansive part of the nature of humans. It is not like the celestial body, where it is an energetic template of your physical body. It is more like a seed of energy for the potential of your sensory experiences. The highest aspect of your intelligence oversees the growth of your karmic body.

Once you have undergone your Kundalini awakening, you have the chance to be free from future karmic disturbances. Karma is a word that denotes the cycle of the causes and effects in your life. Your future will be affected by every action you take in your life. This effect will also apply to your words and thoughts. You possess the power to create experiences that are bad or good. Most people have made poor choices that leave them with an excess of bad karma. These events happen because you let your ego get in the way of your better judgment.

When you have experienced your transformation, your soul is cleansed of all the old experiences that led to your accumulation of bad karma. When your Kundalini is awakening, you will need to learn to let go of your ego, to allow the energy of goodness to flow freely through you. Now that you are cleansed spiritually, you need to keep your karmic slate clean.

Learn to feel gratitude for all of the experiences you have, the bad as well as the good. Try to see the good in every occasion and event in your life. Do not let the actions and attitudes of other people change the way you feel toward the universe, but show your love to everyone. Make sure that the things you do and the things you say are driven by a passion for yourself and others. Negative thoughts will create negative energy and bad karma, so try to keep your attitude well-balanced and happy. You will need to forgive those who hurt or offend you. This forgiveness may be the most challenging part of maintaining a karmic balance, but it is imperative. Abundance and generosity have been given to you by the Kundalini awakening, and you will need to learn to use them.

Open Psychic Ability

After your Kundalini awakening, your psychic abilities will blossom. To achieve a full transformation, all of your chakras must be opened, and that includes the Crown Chakra and the Third Eye Chakra. Your Third Eye is your portal to all things in the astral world, and your Crown Chakra will put you in touch with the divine and higher consciousness.

After your Kundalini awakening, you will notice your increased psychic abilities if you are ready to accept them. At first, you will only see the symptoms that tell you your Third Eye is open, and the psychic abilities are there for you to enjoy. One sign you will notice is an increase in your ability to foresee future events. You might start with a small fluttering or tug in your stomach that tells you something is about to happen. Let your intuition direct you and try not to fear it or ignore it. In the beginning, the feelings may be scary, but realize that you completely control this ability.

You might become more sensitive to changes in light as your Third Eye begins to expand. After the awakening, you will see the world in a new light, and colors will appear more vivid to you. You will collect the benefits of your new heightened view of the world since you are now more in sync with your spiritual side. You will find yourself more loving and forgiving, calmer in your new life. This new calm will allow psychic visions to come forward even faster. Your spiritual powers of intuition now guide changes in your life.

It might seem like a burden to see and know more than other people around you do, but your Third Eye will allow you to see through the illusions and drama in your life. You will make better decisions through your new clarity of thought. And you will have a heightened sense of your inner self. You will begin to see yourself as part of the larger fabric of the universe and not so much as a person with likes and dislikes. You will rely more on yourself with your increased sense of self, and you will begin to enjoy the successful life you always wanted.

Your new life after your Kundalini awakening might feel somewhat like a mid-life crisis. Everything you knew before has been taken away or is dissolving right before your eyes. Your entire life is open for review. Your career, your family connections, your relationships, your dietary habits, all of your old addictions and habits, everything you knew before, and felt comfortable with or understood might now be gone, or it won't mean the same to you. Fear and resistance will stall your transformation process. Your journey is just beginning. Meet your path with courage and conviction.

CHAPTER 6
Kundalini Misconceptions

Kundalini energy is the dormant power of divine infinity in human beings. It is a natural and healthy quality that is driven by your own spiritual energy that removes all duality and suffering from your life. When your Kundalini awakens, you will experience pure consciousness. Your thinking will shift, and you will no longer identify with your mind, but you will now identify with the awareness of the universe around you. Instead of realizing you have thoughts and believing those thoughts, you will shift to a realization that these thoughts are not yours but a product of the drama and illusion around you.

Because of the nature of Kundalini, you do not realize it is there until you awaken it. You might know that everyone is born with it, but until you experience Kundalini, it will have no meaning for your life. When it begins to awaken, you realize there is so much power within you waiting to be used. When your Kundalini is awakened, you will experience miraculous events that you didn't know were possible. Your body will unleash a new level of energy, and you will find that everything within you now behaves in a completely different way.

The heightened state of energy you experience with the Kundalini awakening will provide you with a high state of perception. The entire purpose of awakening your Kundalini is to enhance your perception of the universe around you. When the snake that is uncoiled and reaches the Crown Chakra, your Third Eye will be opened, and you will see all things with great clarity. This clarity brings a new level of perception. Your physical eyes will only know what they see before them, so they are limited in knowing the true meaning of what they see. When the Third

Eye is open it brings a new dimension of perception that helps you see far beyond the limitations of the physical world.

Awakening the Kundalini is awakening a powerful force inside you. To do this means you will need to support yourself entirely in this decision because of the power you will be awakening. It will enable you to discover your real purpose in life and activate your fullest potential. This ancient practice will help you transform your life by channeling the powerful energy that is already inside of you. While the way will bring powerful energy to you, it is not the dangerous unleashing of mystical powers that many people claim it is. The power inside you can be corrupted if you choose to use it the wrong way, but the power itself is neither destructive or harmful. Myths are surrounding this ancient practice that is not true.

Kundalini Awakening Is Dangerous

The energy that is unleashed during a Kundalini awakening is enlightening energy full of love and healing. Awakening your Kundalini is much like opening an electrical current. The room becomes brighter when you flip the light switch to the 'on' position. When you awaken the Kundalini, its energy will surge through the central channel to all parts of your body, bringing brightness and light to all aspects of you. It will revitalize not just the spiritual body but the emotional, mental, and physical body, all at once. The Kundalini energy travels through smaller channels after it fills the central channel, and these smaller channels follow roughly the same path as your physical nervous system does. This path is how the energy flows to all parts of your body.

When you begin to awaken your Kundalini, you do not know how quickly the process will happen, and this is what makes many people believe that awakening is a complicated process.

If the Kundalini awakens rapidly and can't fill the central channel quickly enough to relieve the pressure that has built up, then the energy might flow up the side channels, the Ida and the Pingala. If this happens, you might feel some unexpected and possibly unpleasant symptoms. While you will feel the bliss and ecstasy when the energy fills the central channel, you might also feel the intense side effects of life traveling up the side channels. These symptoms include muscle twitching, physical spasms, and a feeling in inner fire or burning. These can be relieved with a few sessions of yoga or meditation.

Along with the physical symptoms, you might also feel intense emotions. The energy of the Kundalini will break down all of your preconceived notions and long-held ideas that are holding you back. Once these bonds with the past are broken, you will be forced to face all of this old emotional baggage and discard it like the garbage that it is. This experience might mean reliving old events and experiences that brought you pain. Still, you need to eliminate these experiences from your mind and spirit if you want to move forward into your new reality. After the transformation, you will not be burdened by past experiences that brought you pain. These are the experiences that limit your ability to feel and love, make you be addicted to drugs, alcohol, or food, and hold you back from your full potential.

The only real danger in the Kundalini awakening is that you may be forced to face things you have buried because they were painful. If you want to experience the true self-realization that comes from the transformation to your higher self, then you will need to face these pains from your past and eliminate them. This experience might feel dangerous while you have the experience, but it will cleanse your soul and set you free.

You Need Special Training

Awakening the Kundalini is considered to be the core of all spiritual achievements in those that practice Kundalini. Every ancient sage had his method for teaching the awakening to his students. The sage walked a spiritual path of radical enlightenment that gave them the ability to awaken the Kundalini in others. They led the yoga poses, breathing techniques, and meditation to their students to bring them to the ultimate enlightenment by reviving their Kundalini energy.

Using the practice of Kundalini yoga will allow you to open your chakras to release the flow of Kundalini energy through your body. This practice is the ancient science and art that deals with the transformation that will bring you an expansion of consciousness. You will use the energy that is building within you to perform the poses and postures, make the sacred sound of the chanting, learn correct techniques for breathing, and meditate to bring peace and balance to your body and spirit.

Kundalini yoga will help you unite your consciousness with the consciousness of the cosmic by carefully performing the meditations and exercises in their specific combinations and sequences. You will soon become adept at knowing what your body needs and how to do it. You will learn how the energy moves within you and how to channel it where it is needed. This movement will allow you to direct the flow of the energy to awaken and stimulate your chakras, heal others and yourself, and become one with the powers of the universe. While you might want to consult with a yogi at the beginning of your journey, it is not needed, as you will be able to do the process yourself with planning and careful focus to the details of your awakening.

Kundalini Is a Religious Practice

Kundalini is an energy force that rises within you as a result of awakening. This energy will perform many smaller transformations within you that will all lead to the broader change that will bring you to self-realization. Your thought processes, especially the thoughts that bring negativity, will be brought forth for examination. You will be forced to observe these thoughts and the emotions that come from them, you will learn from these thoughts, and then you will learn to let go of them. You will not experience explosive neurological mayhem or strangely altered states of mind. You will begin to enjoy the clarity of mind that will bring you peace, increasing calmness of your spirit and a new sense of empowerment in your daily life.

During your awakening, you might experience periods of altered consciousness. These are ecstatic states of being where you simply go along for the ride. You will calmly observe the changes in your body and mind without reacting to them. This peace is a large part of the process of awakening the Kundalini, learning to be without responding to everything you see and hear. You will realize that the ecstatic experience is not the goal; it is a stepping stone in the transformation process.

Christianity speaks of the goodness of the Holy Spirit working within you. Kundalini speaks of the integrity of the energy rising within you. Kundalini and the Holy Spirit can be thought of as two different names that describe the same thing. The Holy Spirit is thought to be a force of God, showing the power of God in action. Kundalini is also a force of life, bringing its followers to achieve true peace. Both are often described as being the animating or vital force in all living beings. They are the breath of the human. They use their power to perform a transformation within the person to bring them to a higher connection with the divine and the powers of the universe.

Neither has a specific physical form but is seen in the way people imagine them. Humans have their mental image of the Holy Spirit and the Kundalini energy. When you think of their names, the image will come to you. Both images help you understand the teaching of a power that is higher than you, a power that draws you upward to become the best version of yourself possible. Just as the Holy Spirit gives you the ability to fight the things that make you sin, Kundalini energy gives you the power to destroy the old habits in your life that create the desire for you to do things that are bad for you. Both help you fight off the things that are bad for you to help you walk a path of light and goodness. Both the Holy Spirit and the Kundalini energy will remain with you as long as you believe in their power and trust in their abilities.

They will both give you the power to accept adversity as a way of life and not be heavily burdened by it. Both will show you how to make positivity from negativity. Both will encourage you to walk with the Spirit, whichever Spirit you choose to walk with. This means you will not be guided away from the path of goodness and light, you will not succumb to the temptations of evil, and you will keep an open mind and a peaceful spirit within you. Letting the Holy Spirit fill your soul is much like awakening your Kundalini energy. Both will bring you endless happiness. The Holy Spirit becomes active within you when you repent your sins. The Kundalini becomes active within you when you let go of past traumas.

Whether you are picturing the work of God or a god, both schools of thought teach that the name stands for non-duality. Both names stand for the same thing. Non-duality is the absence of a division between the higher power and the human. If you walk with the Holy Spirit inside you, then you are one with God. If you walk with the power of the Kundalini energy awakened inside you, then you are one with the divine. You need to be reborn to walk with the Holy Spirit or experience the transformation that Kundalini energy brings. You must believe in their importance before they will become a part of your life. The non-duality of feeling is the only real truth in life, the one fact that makes all other realities possible.

Kundalini is not technically a religion, although it shares many essential facets of organized religion. But it does bring you to experiences that are similar to those events experienced by religious people. Both Kundalini awakening and Christianity have the same goals and want the same outcome for you. Both will teach you how to let go of your ego and live a life filled with higher purpose so you can reach your real goal and destiny.

Awakening the Kundalini Is Frightening

Many people find the awakening of the Kundalini energy to be a beautiful wave of divinity that opens new sensations and heals their emotional and spiritual wounds. The inner bliss begins at the base of your spine and fills your body with peace and calm. The fear of the Kundalini awakening comes from the changes it causes within you. The specific practices of Kundalini are designed to awaken the energy that will transform your life in many ways.

Some of the sensations you experience during an awakening will include the release of negative thoughts and emotions, feelings of deep connection with the universe, and a physical tingling down your spine. It can be an intensely spiritual and physical experience. The potential energy that is bottled inside your body is released during the awakening and becomes available for you to use. While there are methods for awakening this correctly, it is customary to make mistakes during your awakening. This energy is the part that many people have difficulty with. You will need to be physically and mentally prepared for the changes you will undergo during the transformation.

Some people have compared a Kundalini awakening to sticking your finger into a light socket. Real Kundalini awakening is much like the power of creation so that you might experience something like the Big Bang going off inside your body. During the awakening, you may feel some or all of the various symptoms that might confuse or frighten you. The physical symptoms can include sudden random pain, chills or fever, respiratory problems, sudden jerking in your extremities, strange vibrations from deep inside you, hallucinations and visions, and sudden headaches; the emotional and mental symptoms might include altered states of consciousness, going quickly into a trance, out of body experiences and astral travel, feeling bipolar mood swings, extreme anxiety, paranoia, and intense fear.

It is normal to feel some or all of these symptoms, or you might feel nothing at all. The mistake that some people will make is trying to force the Kundalini awakening before it is ready. While you need to work through the experience, you don't need to rush it. Awakening your Kundalini energy is a new way of life, but it is not a goal you need to strive for. So try not to overstain yourself when you are awakening your Kundalini. Your body needs to be prepared for intense sessions of meditation or yoga poses. Begin slowly and work up to a longer and healthier practice as your body is prepared for it. This fact is also true if you are working on unblocking your chakras to allow the flow of the Kundalini energy. If you encounter any physical, mental, or emotional problems during the process, take a break and come back to the practice when you have allowed your body to rest.

Some people will resort to using drugs or alcohol to speed up the process of awakening the Kundalini. This substance abuse is not recommended for various reasons. The reasoning is that these substances will help calm the mind and the body and allow the awakening to proceed uninterrupted. But it is impossible to truly open the Kundalini properly when you are not entirely aware of your actions.

When Kundalini awakening is attempted the correct way, it is not a frightening experience, other than the physical and emotional symptoms you might experience. The transformation will cleanse old emotional baggage from your soul, and revisiting these experiences may cause pain. But this part of the process is needed to cleanse your soul to allow room for the power of the Kundalini. You can minimize some of these possibly frightening aspects by making sure you are ready for the Kundalini awakening both physically and mentally.

Be in reasonably good health before you begin. Awakening the Kundalini will put some strain on your body and mind. Always begin your practice slowly until you feel you are ready to increase them. Take enough time for yourself during the process so you will be able to rest and relax. During and after the awakening, you will need periods of rest and solitude to help your body maintain its balance. Without this alone time, you may experience some of the adverse side effects. And always remember to practice being grateful for all things and all situations. You need to fill your day with humility, gratitude for your life, and respect for others. This new attitude will help your energy align easily and allow an optimal flow of positive energy.

Kundalini Changes Your Relationships With Other People

Awakening your Kundalini will bring all of your subconscious patterns to the surface so that it might have an enormous impact on your relationships. Your subconscious patterns run underneath the surface of your relationships. They are the factor that will decide whether you will stay in a particular relationship or leave it. It is more difficult to leave the relationships you have created with family members, and these can mask the unhealthy patterns that create unhealthy ways in which you interact with the people in your family.

It can be excruciating for you to let go of particular relationships. Awakening your Kundalini does not mean that all of your relationships will come to an end. The power of the Kundalini energy might mean that you will view your current relationships in new ways. After the awakening, you will possess a broader perspective and further information on the realities of life. You can make conscious choices about the relationships you currently have in your life, deciding if this is someone you need to keep in your life or let go with love and eternal affection.

Your Kundalini awakening will allow you to see if the relationships in your life offer you unconditional support and love. You need to decide if the connections were chosen from the misguided beliefs you once held or some other reason buried deep in your subconscious. Many people choose to remain in relationships for unhealthy reasons:

- Shame or guilt if they leave the person behind
- Desire or need for some kind of security
- Codependency
- A need for validation from an external source
- Obligation
- The fear of being abandoned or alone
- A desire to fit into a group, any group, and not be an outcast
- The need to fix a bad relationship from the past
- Familiarity

Your subconscious thoughts will mirror your current relationships. You might feel obligated to stay with someone who no longer meets your needs. You might fear being alone in life or not being part of the current social scene. Your attachment might be driven by codependency or your need for validation from someone else. You might fear that you can't support yourself on your own, that you need someone else to provide financial security. You might also be repeating unhealthy patterns from a previous relationship with a current relationship. Maybe a current relationship mirrors a toxic relationship from your past, and you remain in it to try to fix the issues. Or a current relationship might feel familiar, although tedious, and you stay in it because resistance would take too much effort.

Awakening your Kundalini will fill you with the power to recognize the truth of your relationships with others. You will be able to see if this is just a pattern playing itself out or an aspect of your subconscious. Then you will use the healing of the Kundalini energy by using your powers of inquisition to inspect the relationship. As unhealthy relationships begin to reveal themselves, you will need to decide the fate of the relationship. If your partner in the relationship is willing to work on the issues that have been identified, then you could possibly save the relationship. Love and unconditional support from a partner can be profoundly healing. But if the connection is toxic or unsafe in any way, you might not be able to remain in the relationship and still heal your mind and spirit. Remain firm in your conviction to disconnect yourself from unhealthy relationships by using all of the support you need.

Some people in your life will not want to see you grow at the accelerated rate the Kundalini awakening will give you. You might need to let these relationships go for your own sake, or at least spend less time with those people. You may feel the need to grieve over the relationships you are leaving behind, and you need to do this for as long as it takes. Losing any connection can be disorienting and painful, especially if some of these are core relationships. Even if you do not completely release the relationship, you might suffer a significant shift in the frequency of the connection. Do not repress any sadness or grief you feel, because the idea is to cleanse yourself of anything that causes you pain in other areas, and this includes your emotions. The love you felt for that person is still there; it is just the physical connection that has been lost. Your grief and pain are valid, even if the relationship was unhealthy in any way. Forgive yourself for choosing to be in a relationship that was not good for you. Forgive yourself for having chosen unwisely. Letting the person go and fully embracing the grief you feel is the only way you can truly heal and begin to form healthy relationships with other people.

Awakening, your Kundalini, will also show you how to establish healthy boundaries in your relationships. Once you see how painful unhealthy boundaries are, you will want healthy boundaries in all current and new relationships. Before the Kundalini awakening, you might have been okay with having few limitations or none at all, but your Kundalini awakening will change that. The awakening will enhance your sense of well-being. You might feel intense physical or emotional pain when you are with those people who violate your boundaries, even if you have previously established none in that relationship. Spending time with those people might leave you feeling drained of energy. You might have issues tolerating people you once accepted without question. These new feelings may confuse you, but it is just your new enhanced sense of self-worth that makes you question your old relationships. This enhancement does not mean that you need to get rid of the relationship, but you might need to establish new boundaries to remain in the relationship comfortably. Then you can keep the person in your life under your terms.

If you grew up without boundaries or you have allowed people to violate yours, it might take you some amount of time to decide what your needs are and how to set boundaries to protect them. You might have learned that using the word 'no' has negative repercussions in your life. You might have known always to please other people first to prevent losing the affection of others, or to keep the peace in the family. Your needs might have taken a back seat in your relationships, and now is the time to change that. You are like a child now, feeling your way in the world. It is a delicate process to untangle your defense mechanisms from what is best for you. You deserve the rewards that a real relationship will bring, and staying in a relationship that isn't good for you is not a real relationship. This process is part of the reason why Kundalini awakening is so essential for you too.

Your Kundalini awakening has given you a new chance at an extraordinary life. Listen to that little voice inside and hear what it is telling you. Take the time to invest in you because you are worthy of the effort. Healing you and integrating the new you into the old life will take some time, and it will not be a painless procedure. But the effort you put into yourself now will all be worth it.

CHAPTER 7
Healing With Kundalini

Awakening your Kundalini is a marvelous tool for healing your body, mind, and spirit. You might feel the healing from the very beginning, or it might take some time for the healing to begin. As you grow deeper in your practice, you will feel a deeper level of healing. As you continue to practice in Kundalini, you might feel you are facing more obstacles and not less, at least in the beginning. But this is perfectly normal as all areas of you strive to get rid of the things that are no longer useful. This process is not a quick fix that will eliminate all of your problems overnight.

When you begin your Kundalini awakening, you might feel worse in the beginning. Your life might become more negative before it becomes positive. This negativity is a temporary issue, and you need to give things time to calm down. You are not regressing in the practice of Kundalini, but you are confronting the problems submerged in the subconscious that is holding you down. You will need to engage these lessons in all areas of your life. Using mantras, meditation, and yoga poses will help you progress in your Kundalini awakening. Commit yourself to your daily practice and be patient. Let yourself feel and see everything you encounter during the awakening. You will not know the path your awakening will take when you begin. Once you uncover one trauma, another one might show itself. You will use your practice to bring all of these shadows into the light where they can be examined and eliminated.

You may circle some issues many times before they are healed or eliminated. Some of your problems are small, and some have been collected and built throughout your life. You might think you have eliminated an issue only to have it recur later. This reappearance does not mean your actions were faulty the first time; this means that the issue has recurred because of a new angle to the problem. You will receive your information in small segments, which makes it easier to deal with. You will need the commitment to remain on the path of self-healing that the Kundalini awakening will bring you. The course will take you to oneness with the divine, and that aspect is rewarding. You will encounter obstacles in the path, but they are all within your control. You might not know the correct direction of the way, but you know what is in your possession. And the path to Kundalini awakening will bring your health in all aspects of your life.

Physical Healing With Kundalini

Awakening your Kundalini will provide you with energy flow to build up stability and strength in your body. Kundalini yoga will allow you to work all of your muscle groups. Unlike other forms of exercise routines for strengthening, yoga uses tension and the weight of your body to strengthen your legs and arms. Certain moves will spread the value of your body evenly between your legs and arms. Poses like crow pose and crane pose will focus more on your arms as it forces them to hold the weight of your body entirely.

Kundalini yoga will enhance the strength of your body beyond strength training. The poses you do will stretch your muscles as you do them. This posturing will increase your overall flexibility, improve your balance, and increase your range of motion. Yoga poses are not aerobic poses, but they are a form of full-body exercise that is low impact. Kundalini yoga helps to boost your immunity while it improves the function of other systems. It will improve your hormone function and balance the operation of your glands. It will also work to restore your energy levels. You will learn to relax your body, which will help to relieve headaches and lower back pain. You will breathe better and sleep better.

Since the awakening will eliminate much of the stress in your life, it will benefit you in physical ways. Stress is known to cause inflammation that will eventually lead to the development of chronic diseases. Your cardiovascular system will benefit from the lowered blood pressure levels that come with less stress. And your awakening will lead you to a higher sense of your self-worth, so you will begin taking better care of yourself. This self-worth can help you eat better, get more exercise, and lose weight.

Mental and Emotional Healing With Kundalini

Awakening your Kundalini will benefit your mental health in numerous ways. The transformation will calm your nervous system, sharpen your powers of concentration and attention, relieve stress, and increase your awareness of the functions of your mind. The energy of the Kundalini will have a positive effect on your mental health. The awakening will have a significant impact on your mental and emotional health, including your mental acuity.

One important consideration is that the awakening will lower or eliminate chronic stress, which is one of the drivers behind most mental and emotional issues. You will learn to improve your mental and emotional moods. One of the things you know during the awakening is keeping your focus in the present. Your future has not yet arrived, and your past is gone and needs to be eliminated. All of the past emotional baggage you carried around before the awakening is destroyed during the transformation. You will bring out all of the issues that are buried in your subconscious, examine them, and gain knowledge from them, and then you will discard them.

Clearing up old emotional and mental debris will provide you with so much clarity in your current life. Memories of the past drive much of the mental and emotional issues that people deal with. You might not consciously remember the event or the experience, but the memory is imprinted on your mind and your emotions, and it dictates how you act today. During the awakening, you will dredge up all of this debris and get rid of it. Doing this will be painful in the beginning, but it will clear out all of the old mental and emotional baggage that weighs you down.

After you have cleaned out your subconscious, you are left with a more extensive awareness of the events of the present. The wild fluctuations of your emotions will be gone, and your mental focus will improve. The emotions that cause stress, fear, anger, regret, and frustration will all be gone.

Before the awakening, you might suffer from low self-esteem, and you might turn to addictive substances to fight your emotional and mental pain. Even if your addiction is not an illegal substance, you remain addicted as a result of feeling bad about yourself. Food is legal, but it can still feed a habit, and you might overeat because you don't care about yourself. Other people might drink alcohol or take illegal drugs or work too much, but addiction is how some people deal with their mental and emotional issues. Awakening the Kundalini will help to eliminate all of that by getting rid of the things that cause you to dislike yourself. Then your mental and emotional health will improve to the point that you will no longer need your addiction to give you the strength to function in your daily life. You will begin to see your self-worth as you realize your connection to the divine and the rest of the universe. You will learn a new side of yourself, one that feels forgiveness and gratitude, one that is filled with empathy for all people.

You will get rid of the dysfunctional habits that drove your former self. Self-improvement will be more comfortable with your new inner strength. The strength you will gain from awakening your Kundalini will help you build awareness of the former destructive tendencies you might have harbored and ways to eliminate them. Your increased feelings of compassion will help to reduce your anger towards yourself and others. As you distance yourself from the drama and illusion that surrounds you, your emotional and mental health will significantly improve.

Spiritual Healing With Kundalini

One of the essential parts of awakening your Kundalini is the ability to strengthen your spiritual self. Before the awakening, you are driven by your ego. The ego is the part of you that is possessive. It is the part that speaks your name, talks about your possessions, or vocalizes what you are thinking. Your base pleasures and negative emotions drive this part of your soul, and its appetite is insatiable. But when the Spirit is awakened within you, it will allow your Higher Self to enter. The spirituality within you is compassionate, neutral, intuitive, understanding, and calm. While your ego will think, your spirituality will know.

When your truth is revealed, and the things that are not true begin to disappear, you will start your enlightenment. Possessing understanding is enlightenment, and the state of being aware of yourself and the world around you is consciousness. The knowledge of awareness is an enlightened consciousness. The philosophy that goes with this carries many different layers of meaning that are infinite. Every individual layer will add shades of nuances, purpose, and depth that will vary between individuals.

When your awakening is complete, you will have access to all of the higher forms of spirituality that were previously closed to you. You will be better able to achieve spiritual awakening. As you open your soul to the influence of the Spirit, you will move far beyond the confines of yourself. Spirituality is the quality of existing beyond the material or physical domain of life.

Spiritual awakening is associated with your soul and your heart. As a process, it is more closely linked to the emotional body of the human. When your truth is revealed through your awakening, and the things in your life that are not true begin to fade away, enlightenment happens. The state of possessing understanding is enlightenment, and the state of being aware of yourself and the world around you is consciousness. So the knowledge of awareness is enlightened consciousness.

The definition of enlightenment will vary among different people because every person is unique, and their own unique experiences in life will shape every person. And your self is linked to the rest of the universe in the weaving of cosmic forces that are well beyond your comprehension. The fact that it is beyond your comprehension is what will form your path to your awareness of the infinite world beyond the physical world. You will permanently be changed fundamentally by your journey of spiritual growth. Your journey to your inner knowledge will lead to your expansion of consciousness and will be very personal. If you examine the rewards of awakening your consciousness based on the reasons why and how it will, then everything will make more sense for you during the awakening.

Before the awakening, you probably spend more time thinking about yourself and everything that makes you the person you are. You spend more time thinking about your beliefs, fears, failures, experiences, successes, triumphs, morality, perspectives, and awareness of yourself. In basic terms, this is what makes you the person that you are. The self of every person is joined in some ways and separate in other ways. And while you might be bound in some ways to every other person in the universe, your journey to enlightened consciousness is a personal one. Whether you call it a spiritual awakening, conscious living, aligned living, or living deliberately, the concept behind them is all the same, and the journey is yours to take alone. The most significant part of the awakening for you is not the destination you will achieve but what you will learn along your journey. If you make progress all about the goal, then you will not only lose much along the way, but you will make your journey toward consciousness awakening much harder than it needs to be. If you focus on the steps necessary to reach the goal and not what you are experiencing along the way, you will eventually achieve the level of transformation you desire. Everyone will begin their journey at a different point, and everyone will travel their path.

When you begin your awakening and declare your objective of seeking enlightened consciousness, if anyone mocks your decision, then that is someone you need to remove from your life. Rid your life of negativity if you want to walk your path with joy. There is the possibility that the negative-thinking people in your life are people who need your help on their journey. While you will walk your own solitary path, other people will cross your path all along the way. Some of the people you meet will need your support, and some will be there to help you. If you can open your higher self to the possibility of helping someone else, then you have taken another step toward your self-enlightenment. Be wary of becoming addicted to the idea of self-help, the search for self-help, but never actually using what you have learned along your path to enlightenment. Do not fill your spiritual awareness with all of the ways enlightenment can be achieved and then never work to achieve it.

You will begin to know things you never knew before. When your consciousness begins to shift during the awakening, you will see that the things that used to have an intense hold on your mind are not as useful anymore. You may feel that your life is spinning out of control when the awakening begins and that things are moving too quickly. The higher truths you will eventually gain will help you to transcend reality as you align your mind and body. You will overcome your limitations and see your life with greater understanding and vision. As you continue your practice, you will see the reality that is hidden behind what you can see with your physical eyes. You will want to explore higher levels of consciousness and learn the metaphysical truths that have been denied to you previously with your limited abilities.

As your spiritual sense is awakened, your astral senses will come alive. The astral senses allow you to tap into the knowledge of the astral plane and all that it offers. You possess five astral senses that mirror your physical senses and allow you to function fully in the astral world. The cosmic sense you will use most often is the cosmic sense of sight, hearing, and feeling. This sense will give you the ability to see things far away and something that might not yet be a reality. You will also see the shadows of events and experiences, especially the shades of past events that cast their shadows of the present time. You will also be able to hear astral vibrations from astral planes that are far away from you. This ability is all possible because your spirituality has expanded through your awakening, to the point that all of the mystic and psychic abilities in the universe are now available to you.

After your awakening, you will probably use your sense of astral feeling more often than all of the others. While you are using your astral feeling, you will have the power to become aware of certain events on the Astral Plane. You might also receive impressions that are happening from a far distance, both emotional and mental feelings. Your astral sense of feeling is more of an awareness of emotion rather than feeling the same passion that is coming from the people or the event. The sentiment is also known as sense, as it is not quite the same as feeling emotions while you are on the physical plane. There are still many instances of active feeling on the astral plane. Empathy will allow you to feel the actual pain of the other entity, and this is known as having sympathy pains or feeling their condition.

While your psychic abilities will develop with your new spirituality during the awakening of your Kundalini, you will need to practice to improve your abilities. You will first learn to concentrate, to hold your attention firmly fixed on one object for a more extended period. When you are first beginning to practice concentration, try testing your powers by concentrating on an item that is familiar to you, like a book or a pencil. Hold the object in your hands, study its details, examine all parts of the object until you have seen and noted every part of it. Now put the item aside and go on about your day. In two or three hours, come back to the object and repeat the exercise, and you will be surprised to see that there are things you will notice the second time that you did not see the first time.

Anything you can do now to extend your psychic abilities will serve to enhance your spiritual growth after the awakening of your Kundalini. With all of the old emotional and mental baggage eliminated, your spirituality can now grow and develop. You will learn how you are connected to the divine and the powers of the universe. You will spend your time living in the present and see past the drama and illusion of everyday matters. Since spiritual growth is one of the most extensive parts of the transformation, full development may take longer to achieve than physical, mental, or emotional growth, but it will come to you in time.

When you awaken your Kundalini, you will begin to live a peace you have never known before. All of the material things that were once so important become less important or non-existent in your new world. You will no longer be driven by the pursuit of goods and monetary wealth, but you will seek higher knowledge and spirituality. You will be driven by the need to do good things for others, which will help you do good things for yourself. You will feel your new connection with all of the souls in the world, and your duty to live your best life so they may live their best life. You will find the divinity within you, that sense that allows you to seek wisdom directly from the divine, and to hear and understand their message to you. This new spirituality will fill you with patience, joy, peacefulness, and happiness as you begin to live your new life filled with energy, focus, creativity, and compassion. You always knew the possibilities for you were endless, and now you have the opportunity to enjoy them.

CONCLUSION

Thank you for making it through to the end of *Kundalini for Beginners*; let's hope it was informative and able to provide you with all of the tools you need to achieve your goals, whatever they may be.

The next step is to begin your own journey to your Kundalini awakening. This is a path you will walk mostly alone, and at times it will seem very lonely, but you will come out on the other side of the awakening transformed into your higher self, with a true sense of self-realization. Along the way you will clear out years of emotional and spiritual garbage that are holding you back from realizing your true potential in life. The Kundalini awakening will bring you to the higher power lying dormant inside of you.

There are many methods for awakening the power of the Kundalini inside you. The best way for you to be successful is to use them all together, in any combination that suits your individual needs. The poses of Kundalini yoga will bring new life to your physical body, eliminating tension and inflammation as it works to strengthen your bones and joints. Your flexibility will be greatly enhanced. Use the tips in this book to unblock your chakras so the energy from the awakening can flow freely through your central channel and reach the peak where it will unite you with the divine. Essential oils and crystals can also help you along the way.

Kundalini awakening should be attempted when you are fully ready for the process and the consequences of your awakening. The transformation will take you to mental and emotional areas you may have not seen in years. It will bring up old feelings and emotions that are blocking the flow of energy through your body. Once you have awakened your Kundalini energy and achieved true self-realization, you will live the ultimate life you have always wanted to live.

Finally, if you found this book useful in any way, a review on Amazon is always appreciated!

DESCRIPTION

Do you spend your days feeling like something is missing in your life? Do you make lists of all of the opportunities you have missed and the disappointments you have felt because of it? Does your energy level drop drastically in the middle of the day? Are you seeking something important in your life, something that will give you the sense that you have a place in this world and you do belong somewhere? Do you want to feel like an essential part of the universe? If any of these sound familiar to you, then this is the book for you.

Kundalini for Beginners is the book that you need to turn your life around. The contents of this book will give you all of the information that you need to awaken your Kundalini energy and send it coursing through your body. Once you have completed your own awakening, you will

- Find the missing purpose in your life
- Take advantage of your opportunities
- Relieve your feelings of disappointment
- Enjoy elevated levels of energy
- Take your place in the universe
- Feel like you belong

The Kundalini energy in your body is locked in a small space at the base of your spine, waiting to be awakened and used to fulfill all of your deepest desires. Everyone is born with the energy of the Kundalini, but it lies dormant until the person makes the conscious decision to awaken it. If you have deficiencies in your present life, then you will definitely benefit from awakening your Kundalini energy. When you complete the transformation, you will know the goodness of

- A calm mind and a peaceful heart
- Clarity of thought with no harboring of old beliefs or feelings
- Renewed interest in the things life offers you
- Increased empathy for the universe and the people around you

You might find it necessary to make specific changes after your Kundalini awakening. Your new awareness of the divine will cause you to look at your present life in a different light. You might find that some things are lacking that you need. You might also find that some of the things you possess are no longer welcome in your life. Changes will be made, and your life will be different. The information in this book will show you the changes you can expect and the changes you may need to make for yourself. All of the sections in this book are filled with the information that you need to work your way entirely through your Kundalini experience.

Once you have completed the awakening process, you will be transformed into your real purpose in life, your true self-realization. This will begin another part of the process, but the information is here in this book to guide you along the path to your higher self. All of these marvelous happenings, and more, are waiting for you at the end of your Kundalini awakening. Buy this book and begin your incredible journey to full self-actualization.

www.ingramcontent.com/pod-product-compliance
Lightning Source LLC
Chambersburg PA
CBHW081347070526
44578CB00005B/762